THE TAUBMAN APPROACH TO PIANO TECHNIQUE

www.mascotbooks.com

The Taubman Approach to Piano Technique: A Comprehensive Guide to Overcome Physical Limitations and Unlock Your Full Pianistic Potential

Second printing. This Mascot Books edition printed in 2025.

For more information, please contact:
Mascot Books, an imprint of Amplify Publishing Group
620 Herndon Parkway, Suite 220
Herndon, VA 20170
info@mascotbooks.com

Library of Congress Control Number: 2023922987

CPSIA Code: PREG0425B

ISBN-13: 978-1-63755-743-3

Printed in China

This is a book of love and gratitude to the genius of Dorothy Taubman, whose findings continually fill me with awe and inspiration. She was the one individual who had the courage and conviction to question what was considered normal, and to systematically investigate what has seemed mysterious and impenetrable for centuries. The results of her questioning and investigations have benefited and continue to benefit pianists worldwide.

THE TAUBMAN APPROACH TO PIANO TECHNIQUE

A Comprehensive Guide to Overcome Physical Limitations and UNLOCK YOUR FULL PIANISTIC POTENTIAL

EDNA GOLANDSKY

TABLE OF CONTENTS

PREFACE

In the late 1960s, while studying for my master's degree in piano performance at the Juilliard School of Music in New York City, I was facing a dilemma. I had been a student at the school since age sixteen, first in the preparatory division, then as an undergraduate in the college. Now in the graduate program, I was beginning to wonder what was next for me. My teachers were encouraging me to pursue a performing career, but despite my deep love for music and for the piano, the idea of practicing many hours a day with little human interaction felt like a form of slavery. I knew that I faced some limitations in my playing, as well as fatigue in my forearm and upper arm. I also suffered from back pain, which at the time I didn't know was related to my playing. In addition, there were pieces that I felt were beyond my capacity to master. Neither the age-old notion that "practice makes perfect" nor my teacher's saying that "practice builds endurance" was entirely convincing. Instead, I had a growing concern that endless hours of practice would not necessarily guarantee a good outcome. I also had the sense that I wanted to do something that was not so centered on me, something that could make a difference for other people.

In the end, it was my roommate who forever changed the course of my life. She was also studying piano at Juilliard and had heard about Dorothy Taubman, a Brooklyn-based piano teacher with a reputation for being able to help her students overcome the fatigue, tension, and pain that many of them were experiencing. Years earlier, Taubman had begun to question traditional methods of teaching. What caused these symptoms in so many talented students? She made it her quest to find out. Through years of painstaking research and investigation, she discovered the precise positions and movements that undergird a natural technique, prevent problems, and allow pianists to play with security and ease.

Having a sharp and analytical mind, my friend was curious enough to start taking lessons with Taubman. It wasn't long before I began to hear a big difference in her playing; I was amazed at her new ability to play pieces that had once been out of her reach.

I was intrigued, but since my own playing was fluent and expressive, and since I had been told that I had a good technique (fast fingers, clear and even passagework), I resisted my friend's invitation to observe one of her lessons. I couldn't imagine another approach that could replace the endless hours of practice that I still wanted to believe would get me to where I wanted to be.

It took much cajoling from my roommate to get me to observe one of her lessons. I finally went, and what I saw was astonishingly different from anything I had ever seen or experienced. The response to any question my friend asked was not the usual "you need to practice more." Instead, Taubman offered physiological explanations for the problem and suggested a solution. My friend would implement her proposed solution, and the problem would be solved in the moment. Amazing! Here at last was a teacher who could accurately diagnose problems and give rational explanations for how to solve them. Seeing and hearing the transformation in that lesson was revolutionary for me. Best of all, instead of rote repetition, practicing could now involve working toward reliable solutions to technical problems.

This was irresistible. I signed up for a few lessons and quickly discovered the reasons for my arm fatigue, back pain, and insecurity in certain passages. I was shown ways of moving at the keyboard that would alleviate all those problems. I also realized that replacing ingrained muscle memory would take some time, so I decided to wait until after graduation to start studying seriously.

Once I started serious study with Taubman, I found the process and the information so fascinating and captivating that I wanted to understand every aspect of her approach. I felt I was using my brain in an entirely new way, one that required a different level of concentration and focus. I caught on quickly, and after about a year I began teaching the technique to others under Taubman's supervision.

Since I wanted other pianists to learn about the Taubman Approach and reap its rewards, I established the Taubman Institute in 1976 with Dorothy Taubman and Enid Stettner. Then, in 2003, I co-founded the Golandsky Institute with John Bloomfield, Robert Durso, and Mary Moran. This allowed me to present year-round seminars and symposia to interested pianists, and to offer training and certification for aspiring Taubman teachers that would standardize the teaching of the Approach at the highest level possible and enable it to expand its reach. Over the years I continued to deepen and refine the Approach, creating a wealth of instructional materials in the process. I had found a way to fulfill my wish to make a difference in the lives of others.

The genius of Dorothy Taubman was her understanding that when we observe a good pianist at the keyboard, beneath the surface lies a hidden world of efficient and natural physical movements. As she once said, "The body is capable of fulfilling all pianistic demands without a violation of its nature if the most efficient ways are used; pain, insecurity, and lack of technical control are symptoms of incoordination rather than a lack of practice, intelligence, or talent."*

* Citations and information from Dorothy Taubman come either directly from her or her writings, or from my notes on our conversations, compiled over the period from 1968 through 2000. Since much of the book is based on these sources, citations and information from her will not be cited further in the text.

Taubman understood that fatigue, tension, and pain are indications that something is wrong, and that the adage "no pain, no gain" leads us astray and should be put to rest. After all, doesn't pain in our daily life indicate that something is wrong? How then could it possibly be a tool for developing a good piano technique?

To understand how things work, we have to look beyond what is immediately visible. Scientists' powerful microscopes enable us to see that everything in nature is made up of small elements that consist of even smaller elements, different from what we observe on the surface. The same is true at the piano, where the combination of many tiny, complex, and interrelated motions beneath the surface comprises a pianist's technique.

Just as we become ill when one bodily organ fails, when one of these coordinated motions is not functioning properly with the others, the playing mechanism suffers. Traditional methods of piano teaching have not been able to address these types of problems because they are based on what we see on the surface—primarily, the movement of the fingers—instead of on the hidden world of coordinated motions.

Dorothy Taubman recognized that human physiology is the same throughout the species and that likewise pianos are all essentially built the same way. She reasoned that if a child prodigy could master difficult pieces of piano repertoire without decades of practicing scales and exercises, then discovering what these prodigies did naturally would enable other children and adults to do the same. Her observations over the course of many years led to the development of an approach to piano technique based on fundamental concepts of alignment and coordination that form the basis for all human motor activity. Taubman identified the precise movements that activate the appropriate muscles and thereby produce efficiency, ease, and freedom in playing for all pianists, which in turn eliminates tension, pain, and injuries.

The Approach not only enables pianists to play scales and arpeggios, leaps, intervals, chords, and octaves with freedom and ease, but also to create great varieties of tone quality so they can express their musical ideas to the fullest extent possible.

There is a tendency for people to stick with teachings that have been passed down over time, even when they yield poor results. Bernardino Ramazzini, an Italian physician, wrote about the connection between faulty movement and injuries as early as 1700 (Franco 2001, 1382). Clara Schumann, the wife of Robert Schumann and an acclaimed virtuoso, wrote in her diary, "Throughout my entire stay in Copenhagen, I always had to tolerate grief and anxiety concerning my fingers, which were constantly inflamed from much playing" (1993, 145). The great early-twentieth-century Polish pianist Ignacy Jan Paderewski wrote, "I had become used to constant and terrifying pain in my arm, and I had learned to play with four fingers only of my right hand. . . . I felt, as did the physicians, that I might never play again" (1938, 221). The celebrated Russian pianist and composer Sergei Rachmaninoff wrote, "I am very tired and my hands hurt . . . The more I get tired, the more pain I have. This means that by the end of the concert season, the pain is almost constant" (Bertennson 1956, 231). Chopin would constantly complain about a weak fourth finger (Holcman 1954, 1, 11, 12). In his diary, Glenn Gould noted a breakdown of control over his hands and lack of coordination (Ostwald 1998, 298). In more recent times, prominent performers such as Leon Fleisher, Gary Graffman, and many others have suffered from pain and injury.

Yet tension, fatigue, pain, and limitations are not inevitable! My goal in writing this book is to describe the rich world of motion that is the Taubman Approach: the proper positions and movements that enable pianists to achieve a new freedom at the keyboard and experience pain-free and tension-free playing that allows for complete musical expression. I want to ensure that a complete description of the Approach, updated and expanded, will be available for current and future generations of pianists. And I want both current and future teachers to not only understand the Approach, but also to learn Taubman Approach pedagogical methods.

While this book focuses on piano technique, much of the material can be a guide to other instrumentalists, as well as anyone who uses a computer, mouse, tablet, or smartphone; the faulty movements that cause problems at the piano lead to problems in these areas also. In fact, these principles are extremely helpful to practitioners of many other professions who encounter similar problems, including writers, gardeners, chefs, jewelry makers, knitters, drivers, bartenders, baristas, dentists, surgeons, violin makers, dog groomers, factory workers, makeup artists, graphic designers, and more. Understanding the correct use of our fingers, hands, and arms in everyday life will keep them—and us—healthy.

This book explains Dorothy Taubman's discoveries in detail, as well as some of my own contributions to this body of knowledge over the last thirty years. Her work has allowed me to open doors to new insights, and these insights are ongoing in my private teaching studio and through the Golandsky Institute, which has brought the Taubman Approach to pianists around the world. Dorothy Taubman's findings continually fill me with awe and inspiration. It's like seeing the hidden treasures of nature. In sharing these treasures with you, my wish is to make the work more accessible to the many people who can reap its benefits.

INTRODUCTION

Starting in the 1940s, Dorothy Taubman began the research and investigations that would ultimately result in the Taubman Approach to piano technique. Over the years, pianists of every level worldwide have used this approach to resolve technical problems and to reach their maximum potential at the instrument. However, this is the first time that a comprehensive exposition of the Taubman Approach and its unique pedagogy has become available to the public in book form.

Chapter 1: Introductory Concepts presents fundamental ideas and defines terms used in the Taubman Approach. The difference between the two states of freedom and relaxation is explained, along with the causes of tension at the piano and the associated continuum of symptoms created thereby. The benefits of the state of freedom are detailed, as well as how this state allows a natural technique to develop. I also discuss the concept of weight, specify where it must be released in order to support the playing fingers, and describe how using gravity minimizes the workload of the muscles involved, creating speed, security, and freedom.

I next explain the fundamental principle underlying this entire body of knowledge: the alignment and coordination of the playing apparatus. The three aspects of coordination of the finger, hand, and forearm with the piano are outlined as they relate to the mechanics of the instrument. I discuss aiming to the point of sound, address the problems caused by keybedding and its antidote, and open the conversation about tone production, including soft and loud playing, with which many pianists struggle.

In **Chapter 2: Basic Positions and Movements**, I describe how to determine the optimal seat height to assist with correct alignment and co-ordination, and the symptoms commonly experienced when sitting too high or too low. I indicate how to determine the distance from the piano, where to sit on the bench, where the feet are located for ease of pedaling, and how to bring the body to the correct point of balance. Having established correct seating, I discuss the muscles located in the fingers, hand, and forearm, outline which are appropriate for playing the piano, and detail the specific movements and associated problems that occur when other muscles are activated. The difference between curling and curving is clarified, along with incorrect thumb movements and knuckle positions, their associated physical symptoms, and how to remedy problems.

I then discuss wrist height, how it may vary depending on context, and issues that arise when the wrist is too high or too low. The role of the elbow in following rather than initiating motion is outlined, along with the problems that occur when the elbow is too far away from the body, too close, or held equidistant from the torso, regardless of the context. I talk about the role of the upper arm, the problems created when it initiates rather than follows, and its ideal state for playing the piano. Finally, I describe the most comfortable and correct position of the torso, its small sideways and in-and-out adjustments, and the proportion of movement between the torso, upper arm, and forearm necessary to allow the playing apparatus to always be in the correct relationship to the keyboard.

Chapter 3: Fundamental Motions offers a deep dive into the central tenets of the Taubman Approach. Forearm *rotation* is the most well-known and also challenging motion associated with the Approach, and is often misunderstood. Single and double rotation are explained in detail, as is the specific timing required, along with an explanation of rotation in both ascending and descending scales, intervals, and chords. Afterward, the steps required for learning and minimizing rotation are reviewed, as well as the huge benefits that result from applying it correctly. Next, both the lateral and vertical motion of the *walking hand and arm* are discussed in depth, as well as how they combine with rotation. I discuss how the walking hand and arm adjusts in scales and arpeggios to let the thumb cross smoothly and comfortably under the fingers and how it combines with rotation in interval and chord playing.

In-and-out motions are the next major topic. I outline why these motions are necessary to avoid potential problems at the piano, and how to apply them to different contexts. The correct timing of in-and-out motions as they combine with rotation and the walking hand and arm is critical.

Shaping is the final topic in this chapter. I define what shaping means in the Taubman Approach, introduce overshapes and undershapes, explain how shaping combines with the other fundamental motions, and describe its technical and interpretative aspects.

Chapter 4: Other Technical Aspects presents other aspects of piano technique that the Taubman Approach covers. In my discussion of *octaves*, I show how the hand can be opened without stretching, and how staccato touch and gravity can be used to minimize effort. I also address traditional and harmful practices commonly taught in octave playing, and how to overcome potential pitfalls. I next discuss legato and staccato *leaps* and explain how to leap with rapidity and security. *Grouping* is a way of organizing material into smaller chunks in order to make passages easier to play. *The interdependence of the hands* is another important concept, especially since many of us are taught to practice with hands separately. I outline both the vertical and horizontal aspects of interdependence, the benefits of learning hands together, and show how an understanding of interdependence can be applied to creating different tonal lines, polyrhythms, legato versus staccato in different hands, and leaps. Lastly, I present the principles of comfortable *fingering* to help a passage feel easier.

Chapter 5: Connecting Technique to Musical Expression provides an overview of the physical elements beneath a compelling performance.

I explain the mechanics of tone production, give an expanded view of the meaning of legato playing, and discuss the role of pedaling and physical shaping in creating a legato effect. I end with a discussion of the importance of rhythm and the role it plays in musical expression.

Chapter 6: Taubman Approach Pedagogy presents factors in learning the Taubman Approach, the different reasons why students come to it, and the elements in the learning process that lead to the best results. I review the obstacles to acquiring a natural and effective piano technique, such as habits and mindsets that can inhibit development, the risks of studying with an unqualified Taubman teacher, and clichés and common prejudices about the Taubman Approach. Following this, I offer some pedagogical insights from my own teaching, such as the processes I employ with new students, and how best to prepare for Taubman lessons. I end the chapter by outlining the challenging process of becoming a Taubman teacher.

I conclude the book with testimonials from pianists past and present who have come to me to learn the Taubman Approach. Their words speak to the efficacy of this approach to piano technique.

The Taubman body of knowledge is so rich in practical and applicable details that using even a few pieces of information can make a big difference in one's technique. However, in order to glean the maximum value from this book it is advisable to start at the beginning. I include video examples to illustrate each aspect of the Approach, and include a QR code and link to access these examples at the end of each chapter.

INTRODUCTORY CONCEPTS

I introduce the Taubman Approach by explaining common terms that have a specific meaning in the Approach. These include concepts such as *freedom versus relaxation*, what the term *weight* refers to within the Approach, and how *gravity* can be used to our advantage. Following this, I introduce the fundamental principles of alignment and coordination that underpin the technique.

FREEDOM VERSUS RELAXATION

Pianists often use the words *freedom* and *relaxation* interchangeably, yet there is a world of difference between these two concepts when it comes to piano technique and to movement in general. To understand the difference between tension and relaxation, it is necessary to understand how muscles work. Limb parts contain two opposing muscles, and at any given moment, these muscle pairs can be in one of three states: relaxation, tension, or freedom.

The state of relaxation. In this state, both sets of opposing muscles are at rest, such as when the body is lying down. However, at the piano the relaxation of both sets of muscles produces lethargy, heaviness, and sluggishness, all of which make quick movement difficult. This is because moving from a relaxed state takes extra effort. Since all motions require muscular activity, total relaxation can never be a solution for piano technique.

The state of tension. In this state, the opposing muscles pull against each other, creating tension. Pianists often equate tension with solidity, yet nowhere in life can we move freely with tension. At the piano, tension typically occurs when the fingers curl, straighten, isolate, or stretch. An example of isolation is when all five fingers are down on the key bottom and one finger is lifting at a time. The tension from these simultaneous opposing muscular pulls results in fatigue, pain, limitation of speed and accuracy, and often injury.

The state of freedom. When one muscle is active and its opposing muscle is passive, tension is eliminated. I call this absence of tension *freedom.* Although we cannot directly control the muscular activity in the fingers, hand, and forearm, moving correctly activates the appropriate corresponding muscles. Feeling solid doesn't come from holding the hand and the arm rigidly but instead through correct positions and movements. Freedom is that intermediate state between tension and relaxation that allows the development of a natural technique. When the fingers, hand, and forearm are properly aligned and moving together, when the fulcrums are all in place, and when the forearm is at the right height, lending its support to the fingers, the opposing muscles are passive, and the result is solidity without tension. The playing apparatus feels secure, alert, and ready to move, and the fingers feel equally strong.

THE CONCEPT OF WEIGHT IN THE TAUBMAN APPROACH

Another misunderstanding about teaching relaxation as a means of eliminating tension is the concept of relaxing weight. Pedagogues have recognized the importance of weight in piano playing for many years (Varro, 1966, 506, and Gieseking, 1972, 106). After observing that playing with isolated fingers resulted in tension, they thought that relaxing the arm might solve the problem. Accordingly, they started teaching relaxing weight from the shoulder, upper arm, and wrist while playing. However, like all other bodily movements, playing requires muscular activity, so relaxing the muscles involved in playing makes playing difficult. While relaxation can give momentary relief from tension, initiating movement when starting from a totally relaxed state requires more effort, and this extra effort results in even greater tension, fatigue, heaviness, and pain. Worse still, the cause of the original tension stemming from finger isolation, curling, stretching, and twisting is not addressed, and that results in even more problems.

The idea that additional weight must supplement finger action is correct: although depressing a key requires only a small amount of weight, the finger cannot supply this weight by itself. However, the weight cannot come from the upper arm, because its excessive weight makes it difficult for the fingers to move. In addition, this limb part is moved by big, sluggish muscles that are not suited for speed. Instead, the weight must come from the forearm, since this limb part has both the weight necessary to overcome key resistance and also the ability to move quickly from key to key.

THE USE OF GRAVITY IN PIANO PLAYING

As we know, gravity affects all movement on the planet. It also plays a crucial role at the piano. If the pianist lifts his or her hand and forearm into the air and lets it fall freely, gravity causes it to fall easily. In contrast, if the pianist actively lifts and lowers the hand and forearm, the movement will be forced and laborious.

We can observe gravity at work in other bodily movements too. For example, when we walk, we first lift the leg and then allow gravity to bring it down as the body follows along; whereas if we intentionally try to lift and lower our legs, walking and running become difficult, if not impossible.

When the finger, hand, and forearm drop freely onto the key as a unit, the force of gravity gives support and weight to the fingers, thereby allowing the pianist to minimize the use of muscular activity. This results in solidity, freedom, and speed.

Having defined the key concepts of freedom versus relaxation, weight, and gravity in the Taubman Approach, we are now able to examine fundamental principles of the work.

BASIC PRINCIPLES OF ALIGNMENT AND COORDINATION

The foundation of the Taubman Approach to piano playing is the concept of alignment and coordination: the proper alignment of the fingers, hand, and forearm, coupled with synchronized and harmonious movements that result in rapid and secure playing. This concept is not new. Yoga, tai chi, and many other movement practices are all based on principles of correct alignment and coordination. The Taubman Approach is unique in that without ignoring the rest of the body, it specifically addresses the body parts that are actively involved in piano playing: the fingers, the hand, and the forearm, which together are called the *playing apparatus.*

To achieve alignment and coordination, the playing apparatus must at all times move together in the same direction and at the same speed. Since it is connected to the rest of the body, the upper arm and torso follow along as well. Since the fingers, hand, and forearm always initiate the movement in playing the piano, they are the leading parts; the upper arm and torso are the following parts.

The upper arm and torso must always remain in the same position relative to the playing apparatus. When the playing apparatus moves to the right, the upper arm and torso follow to the right in small amounts, and when it moves to the left, they follow to the left in small amounts. This allows the playing apparatus to always remain in the best playing position.

COORDINATION WITH THE INSTRUMENT

Correct piano technique employs three types of coordination:

1. The fingers, hand, and forearm must be aligned and coordinated.

2. The two hands must be coordinated when they play together. This is discussed in Chapter 4, in the section on the interdependence of the hands.

3. Finally, the playing apparatus must be coordinated with the keyboard. This coordination refers to the moment when the fingertip touches the key and goes down with it. Correct aiming, timing, key speed, and forearm weight all come into play at this moment.

In order to understand how the playing apparatus coordinates with the keyboard, we first need to understand certain facts about how the piano works.

The point of sound. Early in my training, when Dorothy Taubman asked me, "When you put down the key, do you know at what point sound is produced?" I didn't know what she was talking about or even why it was important. I soon understood that without having a correct answer to this question, all the concepts I discuss in this book can only go so far. I realized that all my piano studies up to that moment had never provided me the answer to this fundamental concept.

Aiming at the point of sound. At the piano, we always need to aim at the point where sound is produced. This point is about three-eighths of an inch below the surface of the keys: it is the point in the descent of a key at which the hammer is triggered to hit the strings and immediately falls back. The descent then continues to the key bottom, where it rests comfortably without pushing or relaxing.

Traditionally, the emphasis has been on aiming at the bottom of the key. However, since sound occurs *before* the key reaches that lowest point, even pushing a small amount on the key bottom is redundant. This is called *keybedding.* The famous piano pedagogue Tobias Matthay realized that expending effort past the point of sound is useless. In 1932, he asserted that keybedding is "the most pernicious of all faults—the fault of applying the muscular impulse intended to produce a tone too late during key-descent to effect its purpose" (161).

Even worse, since the key bottom is similar to a hard floor, pressing on it causes tension and difficulty in moving. The keys feel like hard stones instead of soft and cushiony. Since every action has an equal and opposite reaction, when one hits the keys in this way, the keys hit back, causing calluses, bleeding fingertips, and pain that extends to the rest of the playing apparatus. Furthermore, when the key hits back, it causes the finger to bounce on the key bottom, which slows down the playing. When these problems are exacerbated by isolated, curled, stretched, and tense fingers, it is understandable why pianists often describe the piano as a monster with black and white teeth.

In contrast, when the finger aims at the point of sound and follows through to the key bottom, the feeling is that of solidity without tension, along with a sense of an easy and soft landing. All this makes it possible to move to the next note without restriction.

Releasing from the key bottom. Pianists are often advised to release the fingers as soon as they reach the key bottom, which results in the playing apparatus holding itself up. When the forearm holds itself up while the fingers are trying to put the keys down, these antagonistic forces become a major source of fatigue and tension.

Key speed. Dorothy Taubman made a distinction between the two different speeds involved in piano playing. Horizontal speed refers to how quickly one moves from key to key, which is the speed of the piece. Vertical speed refers to the speed of the key as it plays down. When speaking of vertical speed, the words *slower* and *faster* refer to the microscopic changes in key speed that have a great impact on technique and tone production. It is common knowledge that when the key goes down faster, the volume increases. That means that the key can go down slower as well, in order to produce softer sounds. In making the distinction between the two speeds, Taubman opened the door to many other discoveries.

Soft playing. Many pianists and piano students have problems playing softly. They hold their arms up for fear of sounding too loud, and that leads to tension and lack of control. The way to produce soft sound is not to hold the arm up, but instead, to slow the rate at which the key goes down.

When the finger moves down by itself, it has to go fast into the key in order to overcome its surface resistance, which produces a louder sound. However, when the finger has the support of the forearm, this surface resistance can be overcome with ease. Slowing down the key automatically brings less forearm weight into it. This enables the pianist to play softly with control over every sound.

Loud playing. As I just discussed, playing faster into the keys produces greater volume, but a harsh and ugly tone. Yet a slower key descent leads to less sound. The solution to this dilemma is to combine slightly slower key speed with more forearm weight. This results in a big, rich sound without harshness.

BASIC POSITIONS AND MOVEMENTS

SEAT HEIGHT

A major consideration in establishing the all-important proper alignment is correct seat height; without that, coordination and balance cannot be achieved and maintained, and playing suffers. The forearm and elbow should be at the same level as the surface of the white keys when they are not depressed. Accordingly, it is the length of the upper arm that determines the appropriate seat height. If the upper arm is longer, the seat should be higher to bring the forearm to its proper level. If the upper arm is shorter, the seat should be lower. If the seat cannot be raised sufficiently, pads, pillows, or books may be used to attain the correct height. Conversely, if the seat is too high and cannot be lowered enough, a chair with a flat seat and no armrests should be used. For young children whose feet don't reach the floor, a footstool, books, or pillows under the feet will prevent them from sliding down in order to reach the floor and the pedals.

NEGATIVE CONSEQUENCES OF SITTING TOO HIGH

1. The elbow, forearm, and upper arm are too high over the keyboard, which causes fatigue in the upper arm and deprives the fingers of needed forearm support.

2. The wrist has to drop in order to bring support to the fingers. This destroys the alignment between hand and forearm. Also, the weight of the arm now falls into the wrist, which causes wrist pain, carpal tunnel syndrome, and often backaches.

3. To compensate for the lack of forearm support, the shoulder often drops down, causing pain and tension in the neck and shoulders.

NEGATIVE CONSEQUENCES OF SITTING TOO LOW

1. The weight of the forearm falls backward toward the body, into the wrist and elbow. As a result, the forearm cannot support the fingers in their key descent.

2. The fingers curl as they grab onto the keys in order to stay on them, resulting in tension and reduced speed.

3. The shoulder has to lift to bring the forearm over the fingers, which results in fatigue and pain in the upper arm, neck, shoulder, and back muscles, hindering the pianist's ability to move freely.

4. In order to compensate for the low seat height, the wrist is often held too high and the elbow too low. This combination of high wrist and low elbow breaks the alignment of the hand and forearm, which can cause pain in the wrist and the adjacent part of the forearm.

DISTANCE FROM THE PIANO

Once the seat height is settled, the next consideration is the distance from the piano. The correct distance from the piano depends on the length of the forearm. Sitting too far from the keyboard causes the arm weight to fall backward toward the body and away from the fingers, whereas sitting too close crowds the arms. The best sitting position is at the distance from the piano where the torso and the arms can move without obstruction. For the same reason, the pianist should sit in the middle of the bench, neither on the edge nor too far back. This is true for children as well; either books or a stool should be placed under their feet so they don't slide forward. Finally, the feet should be placed in front of the pedals. This balances the body slightly forward and makes it easy to reach the pedals and to move freely in all directions.

POSITIONS AND MOVEMENTS OF THE FINGERS, ARMS, AND TORSO

This section describes both the correct and incorrect positions and movements of the fingers, arms, and torso. However, it is first necessary to consider the various muscles involved.

THE MUSCLES

Flexor muscles. The flexor muscles are situated on the underside of the forearm and in the palm of the hand. They move the fingers downward from the top hand knuckles. As some of the fastest-moving muscles in the body, they are the most appropriate for playing the piano.

Extensor muscles. The extensors, which lift the fingers up, are situated on the top part of the hand and forearm. Both flexor and extensor muscles are situated in the forearm and hand and pull in opposite directions.

Abductors and adductors. Abductors are the muscles that open the fingers sideways, and adductors are the muscles that bring them together. These muscles are slower than the flexor muscles.

Long flexors. Also situated in the forearm, the long flexors are the muscles that reach from the fingertips to the elbow. They are activated when the fingers curl.

FINGER POSITIONS AND MOVEMENTS

Curling fingers. When we curl our fingers, the long flexor pulls tightly over the wrist and fingers. This restricts their motion, causing tension in the fingers, hand, and forearm, and preventing the entire playing apparatus from moving freely, quickly, and easily.

Straight fingers. In reaction to curling the fingers, people often straighten them, which activates the extensor muscles. However, when the fingers drop down onto the keys, we are using the short, quick flexor muscles. So when we lift and drop with straight fingers, we are using two opposing muscles at the same time. This causes antagonistic muscular pulls that result in tension and limit finger speed. To prevent this, we need to move in a way that activates only one set of muscles.

Correct finger positions and movements. The fingers should neither be curled nor straight, but naturally curved. While curving and curling may look similar, there is a world of difference in the results. The best way to arrive at the correct finger position is to begin by letting the arm fall to the side. Then, bring it up to the piano and let the fingers fall in a natural curve, neither straight nor curled. Moving the fingers in this position activates the short flexors, and because these muscles don't cross the wrist, the movements are free of tension. Even the slightest curling in any finger activates the long flexor, causing the entire playing apparatus to tighten and hampering free finger motion. It is therefore crucial to feel and understand the difference between curling and curving.

Establishing the connection of the fingers to the hand and forearm in order to feel ten equally strong fingers is the first step toward developing a healthy technique. As already mentioned, this is not as simple as it sounds, since the person may have spent years practicing the piano with isolated, curled fingers and breaks in natural alignment. As a result, they may find it difficult to feel the correct alignment right away. I use examples of hand and arm movement from everyday life, showing that it is impossible to pick up a glass of water, a pencil, or any other object with isolated, curled, or straight fingers or a dropped wrist.

Thumb positions and movements. The thumb moves differently from the other four fingers. As discussed before, when the other four fingers play downward, they are moved by the quick flexor muscles. In contrast, when the thumb plays down into the key, it uses the abductor-extensor muscle, which is unsuited for playing. Here are some incorrect thumb movement practices and their consequences:

1. Curling, arching (curving the thumb out in the opposite direction), or straightening can cause problems as well. When the thumb curls, it pulls on the long flexor, and this causes tension all the way up to the elbow, making it difficult for the thumb to move. Another tendency is to straighten the thumb or even to arch it, which also causes tension. Straightening or arching takes place most often when a pianist plays the thumb on a black key, especially in octaves or chords. In these cases, the thumb feels like it is sliding off the key. The solution to curling and arching is to always keep the thumb in its natural curved position, regardless of whether it is playing on a white or black key. When playing octaves or chords, especially on black keys where the hand opens up and the thumb may look a little flatter, it should still remain and feel slightly curved.

   Improper movement of the thumb is not only a problem for pianists. When teaching string players, I have encountered injuries in the bow arm caused by the thumb being pulled all the way over to the ring finger. To cure this problem, all that was necessary was to put the thumb between the index and middle fingers at a maximum.

2. Stretching pulls the thumb away from the hand and the other fingers, often to its extreme range of motion, causing tension and pain. When the thumb is both isolated and stretched, it has no control over key speed and as a result plays into the key too fast, producing unwanted accents. However, when the thumb remains connected to the hand and forearm and plays with rotational motions, it feels as comfortable as the other fingers. The hand can then span distances of any size without having to stretch, key speed can be controlled, and unintentional accents are avoided.

3. Moving the thumb under the hand is often suggested for thumb crossing in scales and arpeggios. However, when the thumb moves under the hand in order to reach the key it is going to play, and especially as it reaches the extreme range of its motion and when it plays down into the key, it activates two opposing muscles. The resulting antagonistic muscular pulls cause tension, discomfort, and often pain. This pain can extend into the wrist and forearm and is a frequent complaint of pianists and other instrumentalists. In addition, bringing the thumb to the extreme end of its range of motion obstructs not only its movement but the movement of the other fingers as well. In contrast, when the thumb is in its natural position next to the second finger, all five fingers can move freely. In the sections on rotation and walking hand and arm in Chapter 3, I describe a gradual motion of the thumb in scale crossing that prevents the activation of the extensor muscles.

4. Another problematic thumb movement is playing it straight down in a way that mimics the motion of the other four fingers, instead of playing it from the side with the aid of rotation. This makes it impossible for the hand to function normally.

5. The thumb has two joints: the nail joint immediately above the thumbnail, and the main thumb knuckle above that. Like the top knuckles of the other four fingers, the main thumb knuckle acts as the fulcrum for thumb motions and aligns with the hand and forearm. Neither the thumb nor the other four fingers use the wrist as a main fulcrum.

When either the nail joint or the top knuckle caves in, the thumb cannot move properly. This collapse, especially of the top knuckle, can often cause backache. Once the teacher corrects these collapses, the thumb can then properly connect to the hand and the forearm.

The problems caused by a collapsed main thumb joint were made clear to me soon after I started teaching the Taubman Approach. A young pianist complained about back pain so severe that she could only play for a few minutes before having to lie down to get relief. I didn't know much at the time, but when I saw the big "dimple" in her thumb joint, I knew that that was the source of the pain. We corrected the position of the thumb joint, and in a short time her backache disappeared.

An especially brutal practice is the attempt to make the hand bigger by physically pushing out the main thumb knuckle and often curling it at the same time. This separates it farther from the other fingers, causing even more tension and pain. Pushing out the main thumb takes isolation to the extreme. Not only is the intentional deformation of the hand of no help in handling large distances and chords, but it is also physically damaging to the thumb and hand.

I once had a student who had been taught to push out the main thumb knuckle to an extreme to make her hand bigger, and the hand actually became deformed. The result was a tremendous amount of tension, difficulty in moving the thumb, and a great deal of pain and suffering. After I worked with her to bring the thumb closer to the second finger, thereby unifying it with the rest of the hand, the hand returned to its natural appearance and became totally functional. It looked and felt so different that the student told me she felt like she had surgery.

As shown above, the solution to these incorrect positions and movements of the thumb is to always keep the thumb in a natural curved position, connected to the hand and forearm just like the other fingers. With the help of rotation, it can then play with ease and efficiency.

KNUCKLE POSITIONS

All movements at the piano are based on the leverage principle. A lever is a rigid body moving around a fixed point, or fulcrum. Everyday examples of levers include cranes, drawbridges, crowbars, and seesaws. In the human body, fulcrums are the basis for the movement of all our limbs. The fulcrums that operate when playing the piano are the top finger knuckles for the movement of the fingers, the wrist for hand motion, the elbow for forearm motion, and the shoulder for upper arm motion.

The top knuckles for the second, third, fourth, and fifth fingers, often called the bridge, are the fulcrums from which the fingers move. The position of the main thumb knuckle was discussed in the preceding section. In order to determine the correct knuckle position for the other four fingers, drop your hand to your side. Then, without changing the positions of the fingers, bring your hand to the keyboard. Note that the top knuckles are neither high nor low, but just slightly higher than the middle knuckles. This natural position of the top knuckles enables the fingers to move freely and should not be altered. When the hand is naturally curved, the top knuckle, the middle knuckle, and the nail joint are all in place.

Here are some typical incorrect knuckle positions:

1. A high bridge. Based on the erroneous assumption that the normal bridge is not strong enough, many teachers recommend a high bridge. However, when the top knuckles are too high, in the shape of a tent, the fingers straighten and the middle knuckle disappears. Since the high bridge brings the fingers into a position where the slightest movement

downward brings them to the limit of their range of motion, the mobility of the fingers becomes limited.

A high bridge creates other problems as well. It restricts the ability of the fingers to open sideways. It also pulls the support of the hand and forearm up and away from the fingers as they play down on the keys. Finally, it destroys the alignment between the fingers and the rest of the hand.

2. A low bridge. Conversely, when the top knuckles are low, relaxed, and look like dimples, they break the connection between the fingers and hand, again making it difficult for the fingers to move. Like all other fulcrum breaks, this break often causes back pain. When I first played for Dorothy Taubman, she asked me if I had a backache, which made me think she was a witch; I wondered how she could possibly know that I had suffered from backaches since childhood. She pointed out to me that my top knuckles and wrist were somewhat low. After I corrected these positions, my backaches completely disappeared.

3. A missing middle knuckle. When the hand is naturally curved, three knuckles are visible: the top knuckle, the middle knuckle, and the nail joint. As previously discussed, if the top knuckles are too high, the fingers straighten and the middle knuckle disappears. This prevents the natural curve of the hand, which is necessary for free finger motion. It also causes another break in the alignment. Accordingly, the middle knuckle should always be visible and consciously felt.

4. A caved-in nail joint. The nail joint often tends to cave in, especially in young children when the fingers are still soft and incompletely formed. Unless and until this tendency is corrected, it will persist indefinitely. The common cure is to compensate by curling the fingers. As previously explained, however, curling causes tension; it thus

> cannot be a good solution. I have observed that in many cases, even after I have the student adopt a naturally curved finger position, the caved-in nail joint is still a problem. Years of curling the fingers have not only increased tension but have not solved the underlying problem; the "solution" of curling the fingers has become so ingrained that it inhibits the real solution. This is a good reminder that forced solutions rarely work long term.

The remedy is for the first joint not to be pushed out or caved in, but to be slightly curved, almost straight-looking, while making sure that the knuckle is present. One way to check that it's strong and not easily caving in is to touch the knuckle lightly and see if it holds. In addition, feeling the sense of contact between the fingertip and the key further strengthens and stabilizes the knuckle. I also make sure that the fingers are properly aligned with the hand and forearm; for the fingers to feel strong, they always need the support of the hand and forearm behind them. Just like correcting other breaks in alignment, correcting the break in the nail joint further solidifies the alignment of all parts and creates a strong foundation for all movements.

WRIST, ARM, AND ELBOW POSITIONS AND MOVEMENTS

The wrist. As the fulcrum for hand motions, the wrist does not move independently but instead responds to the motions of the forearm and the hand as they accommodate different finger lengths and move to shape phrases. To maintain correct wrist height, the wrist must always be at the level where the hand and forearm feel connected to each other. This allows the playing apparatus to move in a unified way. In this basic position, the wrist usually looks slightly higher than the main finger knuckles. It looks more level when playing scale passages and higher when the hand needs to open more, such as when playing large distances, octaves, chords, arpeggios, and large broken intervals.

A low wrist breaks the alignment between the hand and forearm so that it can no longer act as a fulcrum for hand motions. Instead of supporting the fingers, the weight of the forearm falls into the wrist, causing wrist pain and often carpal tunnel syndrome. Also, when the wrist is low, the fingers feel like they are falling off the keys. As a result, they grip the keys, causing tightness in the fingers, hand, and forearm. The back muscles tighten as well, often causing pain.

A wrist that is too high also breaks the alignment between the hand and forearm. It limits finger and hand motions, since even the slightest downward motion brings them to the limit of their range. As discussed in the section on seat height, a high wrist can produce pain in the wrist and in the forearm area close to the wrist. A high wrist also often causes the elbow to drop, which has two consequences. First, the elbow can no longer act as a fulcrum for forearm movements. Second, the weight of the arm falls into the elbow, removing its support from the fingers. This again forces the fingers to grab onto the keys, resulting in tension.

Many pianists come to me with a relaxed wrist. They believe that the wrist needs to relax from the inevitable tension most pianists experience and that it should act as a shock absorber as well. They are also told that a low wrist is necessary for a beautiful, singing tone. The Taubman Approach demonstrates that when the playing is correct, there is no shock to be absorbed. When I initially show people how to drop into the key with each finger, a common response is for the wrist to drop too low. I then show the pianist how to drop into the key without the wrist falling. It has to stop at the height that keeps the hand and forearm connected and unified, without the wrist tightening. As indicated, the correct wrist height also depends on the correct seat height.

When the pianist with a low wrist begins to keep the wrist at the proper height, the common perception is that the wrist feels like a mountain. In reality, the wrist is level: neither too high nor too low. I use a mirror to show the pianist that when the playing apparatus drops into the key with the wrist staying at the right height, it looks level. That helps to align perception with reality. Keeping the hand and forearm aligned by maintaining the wrist at the right height produces solidity and security in playing.

The elbow. The elbow connects the forearm to the upper arm and acts as a fulcrum for forearm motions. When the playing apparatus moves to the right or the left, the elbow follows proportionally, bringing the upper arm with it. To be most effective, the elbow should follow the playing apparatus rather than have it initiate motion on its own. Otherwise, it tends to move too much.

There are limits to how far the elbow should move. When the elbow moves too far away from the body, bringing the upper arm with it, the results are fatigue, tension in the upper arm and neck area, and reduced speed. On the other hand, when the elbow is kept close to the body at all times, it loses its ability to act as a fulcrum for forearm motion. The connection between the forearm and upper arm is lost, restricting the ability to move freely.

Another erroneous practice is to hold the elbows at an equal distance from the torso at all times. This ignores the reality that as the playing apparatus moves into the middle register in front of the body and beyond, the elbow and the upper arm have to come along with it, so they also end up in front of the body. As the right hand moves farther into the lower left-hand register, or the left hand moves into the upper right-hand register, the elbow moves closer toward the belly button. At the same time, the torso moves to the left or right in order to make room for the elbow and the arm. In short, we are always moving and adjusting in accordance with the choreography of the piece.

In a tense technique the elbow often remains rigid, and this rigidity generally extends to the upper arm as well. Elbow tightness affects the freedom of forearm motions. When the removal of forearm and upper arm tightness doesn't free the elbow enough, I suggest that the pianist let go of internal elbow tension without changing the elbow's location in order to achieve freedom for the playing apparatus.

The arm. The arm has two parts: the forearm and the upper arm. The forearm extends from the wrist to the elbow; the upper arm extends from the elbow to the shoulder. Each part has distinct roles. The lighter, quicker forearm moves as fast as the fingers and also has the weight necessary to support them in key descent as well as to provide the power for greater volume. Therefore, it is the role of the forearm to initiate motion and lend weight to support the fingers.

In contrast, the heavy upper arm is moved by slow and sluggish muscles unsuited for rapid movements since they tire easily and quickly. Instead, its role is to serve as a stable point for forearm movements, and to follow the fingers, hand, and forearm so that they can remain unified and comfortable in any register.

As the fingers, hand, and forearm move away from the center of the piano, the upper arm accompanies them in small and appropriate amounts, which avoids excessive and tiring motions. As it returns to the center of the piano, the upper arm again follows the forearm as it comes closer to the body. When the forearm and upper arm move in this way, the feeling of freedom, ease, and lightness in piano playing is assured.

The fact that the two parts of the arm are aligned and move together does not mean that they are equally active, or that they perform similar or equal functions. This fundamental concept may have been overlooked historically because forearm action is small and hard to detect, while upper arm movements are more visible. We can compare the relationship of the upper arm to the forearm with the relationship between the torso and the legs when walking. The torso does not lift the legs and move them forward and down; instead, the legs initiate these motions, and the torso responds with slight vertical and lateral motions. Although the movements all feel like one action in both walking and piano playing, in both cases some parts of the body initiate while other parts follow.

Initiating motion from the upper arm as it moves up and down the keyboard was developed as a response to the notion of "quiet arm and active fingers." This notion produces isolation, twisting, and stretching because it ignores the physiological characteristics of both the upper arm and forearm.

Another common practice used to relieve the tension resulting from an overactive upper arm is relaxing weight from the upper arm and shoulder. This collapses the shoulder fulcrum to which it is connected, as well as the elbow fulcrum, the point from which the forearm moves. These collapsed fulcrums cause tension and pain in the neck and shoulder. Also, when the upper arm relaxes its heavy weight, it becomes difficult for the fingers to move. In this state of relaxation, additional muscular effort is required to initiate motion, which causes more tension as well.

Years ago, my son was preparing for a piano audition at the School for the Performing Arts in Manhattan and complaining of some forearm pain and tension. Despite my personal policy of not teaching my own children, I decided to get involved. His arm felt heavy from too much relaxation, but at the same time his forearm was rigid. I started by freeing his forearm so that it could move more freely and actively. I then added a little more finger action. These two actions removed the heaviness of the upper arm and allowed him to play with far greater freedom. The audition was a success, and he was accepted.

This experience changed my view of how to treat pianists who exhibit excessive relaxation. I discovered that despite this excessive relaxation, most of these pianists still have rigid forearms. To correct this problem, I needed to first free the forearm, just as I had in the case of pianists who exhibited excessive tension.

Free forearm motion depends on an upper arm that is internally free of both tension and heavy relaxation. The sensation should be one of emptiness or hollowness. I call this intermediate state between tension and total relaxation a state of "no tension." How does one reach this state? Sit away from the piano with your hands in your lap. Turn your attention to your upper arm and ask yourself if you feel any tension. If the answer is negative, that is the state of no tension, and it should be the same when placing your hands on the piano. If there is some tension, gently let go of it, just as when you release tension in any other part of the body without collapsing it. This is the ideal state for the upper arm when the pianist is at the piano.

TORSO POSITIONS AND MOVEMENTS

The torso should be straight but not held up. Instead, one should feel a sense of "resting down" without slouching. The torso should be in a comfortable position, leaning slightly forward, and the lower back should be in neither a concave nor a convex position. This way it can move easily as a unit behind the playing apparatus as it moves up and down the keyboard. The torso must always be facing straight ahead, toward the music stand. If it twists to the right or left, this upsets the correct arm balance at the keyboard and can cause pain in the waist area.

The sideways movement of the torso is even smaller than the upper arm motions discussed in the preceding section. That said, it is still significant enough to keep the playing apparatus feeling the same support and balance on the keyboard in every register. If the torso were to remain completely stationary, then the upper arm would have to move by itself as it moves farther away from the body. This causes fatigue and slows down one's playing.

Just as the fingers move in and out and sideways, the torso also has its own combination of small sideways and in-and-out motions as it follows the playing apparatus. It moves slightly inward when we play in the black key area and slightly outward when we play in the white key area. When we play in front of the body, it moves slightly back to make room for the arms and elbow coming in front of the body, always maintaining a feeling of slight forwardness to avoid the sense of falling backwards. When the two hands play simultaneously at the two extreme registers, the torso moves forward to allow the forearms to support the fingers. As the playing apparatus moves toward the extreme upper or lower register, it again follows in small amounts. If there is a feeling of falling over to the right or to the left, the torso again moves slightly forward to avoid the potential fall.

Regardless of whether the torso is moving sideways or in and out, the correct proportion between the movements of the torso, upper arm, and forearm allows the entire playing mechanism to remain in a correct and comfortable relationship to the keyboard.

Finally, the movement of the torso should originate from the buttocks, not from the waist. Moving from the waist is an isolated motion that twists the torso, breaking body alignment and often causing pain in the waist.

This chapter has discussed the role of each part of the playing apparatus—the fingers, wrist, arm, and torso—and the impact of their positions and movements on one's playing. However, it is not only our playing that is affected by the incorrect use of these parts. The problems we develop at the piano often exist in daily activities, such as typing on the computer keyboard or smartphone, using a mouse, or writing by hand. The common denominators between these various activities and the piano are that they all require correct alignment, correct positions, and correct movements.

CHAPTER TWO VIDEO EXAMPLES

To view in-depth video examples for the topics covered in this chapter visit:

www.ednagolandsky.com/chapter-2

Or you can just hold most mobile device cameras over the QR code below and they will instantly pull up the webpage for you:

FUNDAMENTAL MOTIONS

FOREARM ROTATION

The concept of rotation is often the first thing that comes to people's minds when they think of the Taubman Approach. The "mother of all movements," rotation is the fundamental motion necessary for creating an aligned, coordinated, fluid, natural, and symptom-free technique. Without it, a true technical transformation cannot take place. Rotation is the first step necessary for learning and incorporating other motions, and it requires learning a myriad of details in which none are insignificant. It can only be fully understood when it is properly learned, minimized, and integrated with other movements. Then, all the movements together become one organism, which we call technique.

Child prodigies often rotate naturally without realizing what they are doing. Other pianists may instinctively rotate to a degree, and with further understanding and correct application, their technique can advance to a much higher level. Finally, for those pianists who are injured or who have lost their ability to play altogether, rotation is an essential first step to healing.

Traditionally, we have been taught that the way to move from finger to finger is to lift the finger and stretch it to the side to reach the next key. For example, after the second finger plays, the third finger lifts to reach the next key. However, even that small distance causes a stretch. When a larger distance is involved, the finger has to stretch even farther. This lifting and stretching isolates the finger from the hand and forearm and quickly brings it to its extreme range of motion, since the finger can't lift past the top knuckle. Lifting the finger less to avoid the extreme range of motion is not a solution either; the motion is still isolated, even when it is smaller. Stretching to the side uses the slow abductor muscles, which automatically limit speed. Also, activating the abductor muscles along with the flexors when playing causes dual antagonistic pulls that result in fatigue, tension, and pain in the fingers, hand, and forearm. A well-coordinated technique cannot survive these antagonistic pulls.

Long ago, Dorothy Taubman realized that moving the fingers alone was not the way to develop a virtuoso technique. It became clear that there were other limb parts that could move across from finger to finger as quickly as fingers move up and down. She did some tests starting with the hand, which is the limb part closest to the fingers, then the forearm and upper arm. She came to understand that

1. moving the hand by itself from side to side from the wrist fulcrum was too slow and caused the hand to twist, resulting in wrist pain and often ganglia,

2. moving the forearm sideways was faster than hand motion but still didn't match finger speed, and

3. moving the upper arm sideways uses slow and sluggish muscles that become easily fatigued.

With further testing Taubman discovered that the only motion that matches finger speed is forearm rotation. Forearm rotation eliminates the tension-producing antagonistic pulls by aligning and synchronizing the fingers, hand, and forearm as they move across from finger to finger, thus removing the obstacles to fast playing.

Rotation consists of two motions: a preparatory motion and a swing back to play the next note. The preparatory motion is always in the opposite direction of the note to be played. For example, when the second finger goes to the third finger in the right hand, after the second finger plays with the forearm balanced over it, the third, fourth, and fifth fingers turn to the left along with the hand and forearm. This is the preparatory motion. As the forearm and hand turn, the top finger knuckles turn with them; this allows the fingers to move freely and avoids the limitation of those knuckles. However, the fingers should not lift so much that they separate from the hand. Immediately following the preparatory motion, the fingers, hand, and forearm turn back together to the right to play the third finger, with the forearm supporting the third finger as it plays. This is the swing back, the second part of the rotation. This coordinated motion prevents the dual antagonistic pulls that occur when fingers move by themselves and stretch sideways. Turning this way also minimizes the use of the finger extensors as they lift, and allows the freer and faster finger flexors to move back to play the next key.

Although the preparatory motion and the swing back move in opposite directions, they must be experienced as one continuous fluid motion. If the student has difficulty playing the preparatory motion, that could be because either (a) the fingers, hand, and forearm are not properly aligned, (b) there is a pushing down and pivoting on the finger that just played to create the next motion, or (c) the forearm is simply not sufficiently free.

Simultaneous with the third finger playing, the second finger releases from its key and, along with the thumb, moves closer to the third finger. This eliminates stretching in the other direction as well. In addition, as the forearm rotates back to play the next key, it gives the necessary support and weight to the third finger. This eliminates the need for the finger to press down on the key, which causes tension and often pain in the underside of the forearm.

In the first phase of learning to rotate, when the motions are exaggerated and slowed down, the notes can sound static and identical, prompting people to wonder how one can play fast or achieve any kind of musical expression using this approach. This is a concern I address in the sections on shaping and tone production. But even in this early learning phase, rotation enables the person to start to feel the playing mechanism moving in a coordinated way, with freedom, ease, and with all ten fingers feeling equally strong. This in itself is a huge accomplishment.

SINGLE ROTATION*

There are two kinds of rotation—single and double rotation—and each is comprised of a preparatory motion and a swing back. In single rotation, the fingers rotate in opposite directions to each other, but the playing of a finger and the subsequent preparatory motion to the next finger are both in the same direction. A good example of single rotation is a trill. In the trill with the second and third fingers of the right hand, the second finger, along with the hand and forearm, first rotates to the left to play the key and then continues to turn to the left, forming the preparatory motion to play the third finger. The third finger then turns back to the right to play and then continues further to the right, forming the preparatory motion to again play the second finger. These movements continue for the duration of the trill. As the distance between the two notes of a trill becomes greater, the rotation

* Although I speak of finger movement when describing rotation, the finger always moves with the hand and forearm; so *finger* always refers to the entire playing apparatus, both in this and other chapters.

increases proportionately to allow the forearm to move across the distance.

Although these motions feel continuous, there is a split second in which the playing of the key is experienced vertically before continuing to turn further. This prevents a general rolling back and forth in an exaggerated manner, which can result in a feeling of instability. In the end, however, there is only a sense of a fluid nonstop movement between the playing fingers.

Finally, all rotations from the thumb and from the fifth finger to other fingers are single rotations. The only exception is when the thumb or the fifth finger repeats itself, which results in a double rotation.

DOUBLE ROTATION

Double rotation occurs when the fingers are moving consecutively in the same direction. In contrast to single rotation where the preparatory motion is in the same direction to the last finger played, in double rotation the preparatory motion is in the opposite direction to the last finger played. In the example of a double rotation from the second finger to the third finger, after the second finger plays straight down, the preparatory motion to the third finger is a turn to the left. This preparatory motion to the left is now followed by a swing back to the right to play the third finger. The same motions take place with subsequent double rotations. The next preparatory motion and the swing back to the next note should be experienced as one uninterrupted motion.

A five-finger passage in the right hand is a good example of how single and double rotation work in a group of notes. Going from the thumb to the second finger is a single rotation. The rotations from the second to the third finger, the third to the fourth finger, and the fourth to the fifth finger are all double rotations. When descending, the rotation from the fifth finger back to the fourth is a single rotation, and the rest of the rotations are double rotations.

In a typical scale passage, the rotation from the third finger as it crosses to the thumb is a single rotation, followed by another single rotation from the thumb to the second finger. The succeeding rotations are the same as described in the five-finger example.

The crossing from the fourth finger to the thumb in scale passages that start the second octave is also a single rotation, again followed by another single rotation from the thumb to the second finger. Similarly, in descending scales, the crossing from the thumb to the next finger is a single rotation that is followed by another single rotation.

In both single and double rotation, the finger that has just played releases closer to the next finger as that finger plays. This allows the weight of the forearm to fully transfer its support to the next finger.

After crossing to the thumb. In ascending scales with the right hand or in descending scales with the left hand, once the thumb has crossed over and landed on the next key in the right hand, the rotation continues to the left, or, in the left hand, the rotation continues to the right, forming a single rotation to the next key. Often, when the thumb plays after the crossing, the other fingers have the incorrect tendency to either remain too far to the left to rotate smoothly to the next finger or to "straighten" by pulling the hand over to the right, causing a twist. Instead, the fingers, hand, and forearm should be directly over the thumb, with a slight turn to the left, in a position to rotate to the second finger. This position is identical to the beginning of a scale.

Rotation in repeated notes. Single and double rotation function in the same way when different fingers play the same note. For example, when the thumb plays, followed by the third and second fingers and continuing back to the thumb all on the same note, the thumb to the third finger and the third finger to the second finger are both single rotations, and the second finger to the thumb is a double rotation.

Rotation with intervals and chords. When playing intervals and chords, the forearm always rotates in the direction of the thumb: to the left in the right hand and to the right in the left hand. The landing should put the forearm equally behind all the fingers. The tendency of students is to tilt too far in the direction of the thumb. When this occurs, the hand is not equally balanced behind the fingers.

In the case of an interval or chord going to a single note inside the interval, the rotation is a single rotation from the thumb side to the single note. For example, in the interval between C and the A above it, with the thumb playing C and the fifth finger playing the A, the rotation is from the left to the right when the second finger goes to the E in the middle.

THE TIMING OF SINGLE AND DOUBLE ROTATION

The timing of a single rotation is different from that of a double rotation. Whereas single rotation continues past the finger played to form the next preparatory motion without stopping, in double rotation the playing has to come to a complete stop before the next preparatory motion takes place. Otherwise, the rotation ends up being backwards, since the arm doesn't stop long enough to finish playing the key before the next preparatory motion takes place. To correct this, in the initial training it helps to stop twice as long on the key just played before rotating to the next key. This can be accomplished by saying a one-syllable word like *turn* for the preparatory motion and a two-syllable word like *finish* for the landing. This establishes the sense of playing and completing each key. As the motions between the fingers become minimized and begin to occur automatically, all we sense is a solid landing on each finger.

Because the size of the required rotation to go from key to key is so small when minimized, in the end it is hardly felt. This leads students to worry that they will lose the rotation, especially as playing gets faster. If this occurs, I ask them to compare the feeling before they learned to rotate with the feeling afterward, which is completely different. Speed has traditionally been equated with fast fingers. However, in reality, it is the quick forearm rotational motions that create speed by bringing the fingers to the next key without activating the slow abductor muscles.

I also watch to ensure that the increased speed doesn't cause the fingers to take over, move faster, and wind up getting ahead of the arm.

LEARNING HOW TO ROTATE

There are complexities to both learning and teaching this skill. Here's how I approach some of these complexities, starting with the first steps I take when someone starts lessons with me.

Preliminary steps. Many pianists feel a lot of tightness in their playing. The first step to eliminating this is to free the forearm.* To accomplish that:

1. Let the forearm fall freely to the side of the body.
2. Bring it in front of the chest, with the bottom of the forearm and hand facing the floor.
3. Turn or rotate the forearm and hand so that they alternatively face the chest and the floor. Repeat this motion several times, making sure that the hand remains connected to the arm and doesn't drop down from the wrist.

The fingers should be in a natural position, neither curled nor straight. If it is necessary to further release the inner tightening of the forearm, let the hand and forearm drop freely onto the lap and repeat this dropping motion several times. Dropping helps to "unfreeze" the forearm, a body part that pianists are generally not consciously aware of. It is done with the help of gravity.† The teacher should help the student feel this sensation of free release, which needs to be experienced and cultivated until it becomes second nature. As opposed to total relaxation, this freedom is critical. It fuels not only rotation but all the other movements as well, and thus affects the entire technique. In fact,

* For more information, see the section on freedom versus relaxation in Chapter 1.

† For more information, see the section on gravity in Chapter 1.

in all daily activities in which the hands are used (i.e., in virtually all human activity) these limb parts need to function with this same alignment and freedom. Failing to do so can lead to problems in life as well as at the piano.

Rotating at the piano. The next step is to bring this feeling of freedom to the piano. Dropping the forearm behind the fingers when playing a key is a smaller motion than dropping the forearm into the lap, but it must be equally free. I give this exercise first so that the student experiences the forearm landing freely behind each finger while maintaining the correct wrist height, and with just the small amount of weight necessary to put the key down with ease. The forearm should not drop from an excessive height, but initially from two to three inches above the key and eventually from close to the key. It is only necessary to practice this activity in the beginning.

Once the forearm is free and all the fingers feel equally strong, rotational motion is the way to connect one finger to the next. Since words can only go so far, rotation needs to be physically experienced in order to be truly understood. As mentioned earlier, when people start training in this work, the forearm, which is the rotational engine, is usually tight and unresponsive. As a result, when rotation is first introduced, it typically needs to be exaggerated in order to be felt. Once rotation becomes a habit and the correct proportion of movement between the fingers, hand, and forearm is established, the next step is to minimize these motions in order to play rapidly and combine them with other movements. In some cases, students feel better from the beginning with smaller rotational motions, so the large ones are unnecessary.

Even when the pianist consciously practices freeing the forearm, some tension may remain. The simple act of looking at the forearm as it rotates helps to free it further. It is important to look from the corner of the eye so that the head doesn't turn too far, isolating it from the neck and causing neck ache.

Rotation is the only motion that should be exaggerated when it is first being learned. The walking hand and arm, in-and-out, and shaping motions discussed in following chapters should be taught with the correct proportions from the beginning, since exaggerating them causes problems.

PROPORTION OF MOTION BETWEEN THE FINGER AND THE FOREARM

Achieving the correct proportion of motion between the fingers, hand, and forearm is another important element in minimizing rotation. Due to the strong emphasis on the forearm in the beginning stage, students often ask, "Does the arm move the fingers, or do the fingers move the arm?" This question highlights the difference between the learning process and the end result. For most people, it works best to feel the initiation of the movement from the forearm. Occasionally, initiating the movement from the fingers while feeling the response of the forearm all the way to the elbow works best. As previously explained, we start with the forearm because it is the gateway to freeing the fingers. This leads to the impression that only the forearm is moving. However, the intention is not to replace finger motion, but on the contrary to facilitate it, and that can only happen when the fingers are correctly connected to the hand and forearm. When the forearm turns together with the fingers, there is a sense that the fingers are being lifted and then dropped back onto the key, thus eliminating isolating and stretching. Although the perception may be that the fingers are not moving at all, in reality they do. The difference is that the connection to the hand and forearm has removed the burden from the overworked fingers. They still move, but now in a new and effortless way.

If the fingers become too inactive and the student complains of feeling that his or her fingers are limp ("spaghetti fingers"), then some finger motion should be added. Like adding a spice to a dish, it's best to add only a little to see if it's enough. As humans, we tend to go to extremes, and since motions at the piano are extremely small, it is easy to move too far. If too much finger motion is added, the fingers quickly become separated from the hand, and alignment is lost. The finger action should be just enough to feel the ease of motion while remaining connected to the hand and forearm. There may be some back-and-forth adjustments between the fingers and the forearm until the correct balance is established.

If the student still worries that the fingers are not moving enough, but I see that they are, I bring back the mirror so that they can see how much they are moving. With forearm rotation and without isolation and stretching, the fingers feel like they are *being moved.* As a result, there is no feeling of effort. It's a strange new sensation, but people quickly become accustomed to this wonderful world of effortless movement. Establishing this delicate balance between the finger and the forearm, along with minimizing rotation and integrating it with the other movements, results in speed. This usually occurs on its own; when it doesn't, the teacher can help.

Teaching rotation requires a skilled and experienced teacher, since many situations can occur during the learning process. In the following section, I discuss issues that typically come up, followed by pedagogical insights about this first phase of learning. I end with a summary of the multiple benefits of learning this important skill.

The problem of weak fingers. The feeling of weakness in a finger is not a sign that the finger is intrinsically weak. Instead, it is the result of a lack of connection between the fingers, hand, and especially the forearm. When the fingers move by themselves, they don't have the forearm support that gives them strength. Forearm rotation gives the fingers the support they need to feel strong; this automatically solves the notorious problems of the so-called weak fourth and often fifth finger, as well as "shaky" fingers.

The importance of the nonplaying fingers. The nonplaying fingers play a critical role in a coordinated technique. We normally concentrate on the playing fingers and are unaware of what is happening with the fingers that don't play, until there is a problem. Often there is too much arm weight behind the nonplaying fingers. This both makes unwanted keys go down and also removes support from the playing finger. This is another reason for the problem of weak and shaky fingers. The nonplaying fingers should neither be holding themselves up nor resting heavily on the keys. Instead, they should have a feeling of light hovering or lightly touching the nonplaying keys.

Crowding. Crowding occurs when two non-adjacent fingers (e.g., the first and fifth fingers) have to play one after the other on the same key or a nearby key. When stretching, muscles pull outward, but when crowding, muscles pull inward. Both are uncomfortable and cause problems. Rotation is one of the main ways to solve the problem of crowding. The preparatory motion moves all the fingers away from the next finger to be played. The swing back and the immediate release of the finished finger prevent the two fingers from coming into close contact with each other.

PEDAGOGICAL INSIGHTS

The first phase of learning and applying rotation is often the most challenging since this is when so many changes take place. Rotation requires learning a set of new habits to replace unworkable ones deeply ingrained over years. In the beginning, rotation tends to combine with poor habits such as a tight forearm and fingers, curling, low wrist, and twisting. Until these flaws are corrected, rotation cannot function properly and may even cause more problems. The experienced teacher should diagnose the student's basic technical flaws and oversee the process of correcting them before adding rotation.

The time it takes to master rotation depends on the seriousness of a student's problems and his or her openness to learning new strategies. Additionally, the details and precision of the Approach require a high level of concentration and patience from the student. As progress takes place, the student begins to see the light at the end of the tunnel, and additional progress becomes easier. The expertise of the teacher is critical; if the student is properly applying what is taught and sees little improvement over time, it may be advisable to look for a Taubman teacher with a strong track record. The Golandsky Institute offers a rigorous training program leading to certification and a list of certified teachers on its website.

BENEFITS OF LEARNING FOREARM ROTATION

Among the many positive effects that result from mastering rotation are the following:

1. It relieves fatigue, tension, and pain in the fingers, hand, and forearm.

2. It allows the playing apparatus to be truly aligned as it moves across the keyboard.

3. It is the route to a new definition of what finger independence means. When the fingers are not isolated but connected with the hand and forearm, they have freedom of motion without constraint, and feel independent in an entirely new way.

4. It allows us to move over small and great distances from finger to finger without stretching or missing notes.

5. It is the first step to learning how to produce a thicker and rounder sound.

6. It is the first step to playing without limitations, with ease, and with "time to kill" even at great speeds. Like the roots of a tree, correctly learned rotation is the foundation for the health and longevity of a natural technique.

THE WALKING HAND AND ARM

In the process of teaching rotation, Taubman noted that while the rotational motions greatly improved her students' playing, some improved more than others. Since they were all gifted, serious piano students, instead of blaming the lack of progress on lack of talent or insufficient practice, she surmised that perhaps rotation included another motion that naturally occurred in some people's techniques and not in others. That led to her discovery that forearm rotation combines with lateral and vertical motions of the forearm. She called these motions the *walking hand and arm* since they imitate walking. So, when we say *rotation*, the word automatically includes the walking hand and arm motion as well. The two work together as one.

When rotating, the forearm turns to the left and to the right on a static axis. However, piano playing is anything but static. Vertical and horizontal motions are both necessary. As we rotate to play a note, the free settling down of the hand and forearm behind the finger gives it the support and weight necessary to play the key. This is the vertical component of the walking hand and arm. This free settling down creates the momentum that slightly moves the forearm up so that it can move across and down into the next key. This is the horizontal component of the walking hand and arm. These motions often occur naturally when learning rotation with a free forearm.

The walking hand and arm resembles walking. When we walk, the downward motion of the leg, with the body settling behind it, provides the momentum for a slight motion up, which makes it possible to move forward. Without this upward release, which is so slight that we are generally unaware of it, we would be shuffling instead of walking.

At the piano, the conscious sensation is mostly that of down, across, and down. Upward motion should be added only when the forearm is unresponsive, and then only just enough to allow the fingers, hand, and forearm to move across to the next key. Too much of a release from the key bottom compromises the sense of legato on the key bottom and also causes the feeling of hovering, or holding up, which is tiring and gets in the way of speed.

The reason why the walking hand and arm needs to be combined with rotation is that by itself, it is not as fast as rotation. The rapid rotational motion initiates and carries the walking hand and arm with it. Rotation provides the speed while the walking hand and arm supplies the movement down, up, and across. In this way, they form a necessary and successful partnership. When the two motions partner in this way and become minimized, the fingers can move from key to key at any distance with great speed and security, regardless of hand size.

Finally, there is a specific timing for combining rotation and walking hand and arm. Following the preparatory motion, the walking hand and arm movement takes place with the second part of the rotation, as the hand and forearm swing back to play the next key. In the end, the main sensation is that of a slight shift of the forearm weight behind each playing finger.

Whereas it is necessary to learn to rotate on every note, the walking hand and arm should be used sparingly, and only when it is missing. For example, larger distances, such as arpeggios, leaps, and broken octaves, require increased lateral forearm movement, just enough to arrive comfortably at the next note without stretching. If the lateral motion is too big, it can erase rotation, become laborious and fatiguing, and slow down the playing.

WALKING HAND AND ARM AND ROTATION IN SCALES*

Although the forearm moves only small distances over a five-finger pattern, the distances become somewhat greater with scales, due to the thumb crossing. When crossing to the thumb, the forearm needs to move a full three keys away in order to bring the thumb to its next key, and as a result the lateral shift of the walking hand and arm becomes more conscious and visible. To see and feel the distance that the thumb has to travel, place your thumb with the hand and forearm behind it on middle C, then move your thumb and forearm over to the F, keeping the hand and forearm together. The hand and forearm are now much farther away from the C than in the five-finger example.

* In this section as elsewhere, any example presented for the right hand can be mirrored in the left hand.

For the comfortable and reliable legato crossing in scales that is necessary for security and evenness, the forearm has to move gradually and incrementally. As we rotate from the thumb to the second finger, then to the third, then crossing from either the third or fourth finger to the thumb, the forearm (along with the hand) moves incrementally along with each finger. The correct amount of lateral forearm movement brings the thumb gradually across the keys and closer to the key it has to play, in precisely measured amounts. By the time the forearm gets to the key before the thumb, a small single rotation combined with a small walking hand and arm movement easily completes the task of crossing over to play the key with the thumb. To get a sense of the correct forearm position when crossing to the thumb, play the E–F interval with the third finger on the E and the thumb on the F in its crossed-over position, and note how far out the forearm, elbow, and upper arm are from the body. Also note that the torso has moved along as well.

At the same time that the forearm is moving, the thumb moves in precisely measured amounts as well. When the second finger plays, the thumb moves directly behind it, and when the third finger plays, as it rotates to cross over, the thumb moves behind that finger as well. In this way the thumb is in the perfect position to play the next key. When crossing from the fourth finger to the thumb, the thumb again moves directly behind the second finger, and then directly behind the third finger. However, when the fourth finger rotates, the thumb moves only to the inner side of that finger, since if the thumb were to move further behind the fourth finger, it would arrive at its extreme range of motion.

When the forearm doesn't move gradually and stays behind, it obstructs the thumb from smoothly reaching the next key it needs to play, causing a motion that is too large for comfort and speed, and disrupts the smoothness and evenness of the scale. On the other hand, if the forearm, elbow, and upper arm move too far past the playing fingers, they pull the fingers beyond where they have to play. These excessively large motions are awkward and inefficient and contribute to the loss of rotation and speed. However, when rotation is properly combined with walking hand and arm and the forearm moves in proper increments, the motions become smaller, more precise, and efficient. The fingers, hand, and forearm begin to feel like they automatically arrive at the right place.

If scales still don't feel easy, I suggest that the student examine the following:

1. Is the chair or bench at the right height?
2. Is the wrist at the proper height to properly connect the hand to the forearm?
3. Is the arm balancing directly over the fingers rather than falling back toward the body?
4. Are the fingers too curled or too straight?
5. Is there any stretching? Are the thumb and fifth fingers pulling away from the other fingers? This is a common problem.
6. Are the elbows too far out or too far in?
7. Is the rotation properly executed?

Technique is an integrated system, and success depends on each part doing its job properly.

WALKING HAND AND ARM AND ROTATION IN ARPEGGIOS

In arpeggio playing, a similar process takes place as in scales. However, since the distances between the keys are larger, rotation and walking hand and arm movements need to adjust accordingly. The size of the preparatory motion needs to be slightly larger to precisely correspond to the distance to the next key. At first, and especially in larger distances, a preparatory motion in the opposite direction to where we are going may seem counterintuitive. However, the speed, lack of tension, and feeling of naturalness that result from handling it properly prove its effectiveness. For example, playing the C, E, G, and C keys with the right-hand first, second, third, and fifth fingers requires a little larger sideways movement than playing five adjacent keys (C, D, E, F, G). The preparatory motion to travel from the thumb on C to the second finger on E in the arpeggio is slightly larger than the motion from the thumb on C to the second finger on D in the scale. This is the same for the rest of the notes in the arpeggio, and is another example of how rotation and walking hand and arm work together.

Thumb crossing in arpeggios. Crossing to the thumb in arpeggios is the same as in scale crossing, except that again the movements need to correspond to the larger distances. Correct rotation in combination with the walking hand and arm make it possible to connect the thumb to the previous note. This is imperative for security and evenness. Just as in scales, rotation together with the walking hand and arm bring the thumb close to where it has to play. Then, a small single rotation along with a small walking hand and arm motion brings the thumb smoothly and easily to its destination.

In arpeggios just as in scales, the thumb has to move behind the playing fingers in correspondingly precise amounts to facilitate thumb crossing. This minimizes the sideways motion of the forearm and thus achieves optimal speed and smoothness. Once we add in-and-out and shaping motions to forearm rotation and walking hand and arm, all the motions become even smaller.

Since we are not accustomed to the idea that the hand and forearm always have to move in order to accompany the fingers and stay connected to them, a common reaction to thumb crossings in scales and arpeggios is, "Do I need to move over that much?" The answer is yes. This is the only way to achieve a true legato in crossing to the thumb and is necessary for security and evenness in arpeggio playing. The upper arm and torso have to follow the playing apparatus the precise amount that allows the forearm to be in the right place for the crossing.

Descending right-hand scales and arpeggios and ascending left-hand scales and arpeggios. In ascending passages, thumb crossings often require a conscious motion of the forearm. In contrast, descending scales and arpeggios are simpler and easier since the forearm is moving closer to the body with each finger as it plays. The single rotation together with the walking hand and arm that occurs when crossing from the thumb to the next finger is usually sufficient to get the playing apparatus over to the next key. The single rotation that follows brings the forearm even further over and closer to the body.

Typical situations when crossing to and from the thumb cannot be connected. When the distance of crossing to the thumb is greater than a fourth, the same instructions are followed as in scale and arpeggio playing, except that there is a slight disconnection during the crossing. The feeling is still almost that of legato. Trying to physically connect in this situation would necessitate too large a sideways motion, which is not only uncomfortable but hinders speed and smoothness of motion. It is impossible to connect the fifth finger to the thumb or the thumb to the fifth finger under any circumstances, since the crossover movement would require an arm movement that is too large for speed and comfort. Also, the first and fifth fingers would become crowded. Finally, crossing to and from the thumb as it plays on a black key or in the black key area often requires a disconnection from the previous finger.

UPWARD AND DOWNWARD MOTIONS OF THE WALKING HAND AND ARM

So far, in discussing scale and arpeggio playing, I have primarily concentrated on the sideways motions of the walking hand and arm in spanning distances and crossing to and from the thumb. I will now discuss where the upward and downward motions of the walking hand and arm play a major role, such as when moving from a white key to a black key, in intervals, and in chord playing.

When moving from a white key to a black key, such as going from the second finger on F to the third finger on F-sharp, since black keys are higher, the common tendency is to play downward on the white key and upward on the black key. This leads to a pull between these two fingers and a sensation of climbing up to the higher black key that results in a general feeling of discomfort. For a technique to function well, the keys must all feel as if they are on the same level. This is accomplished by playing down both on the second finger as it plays the F and on the third finger as it plays the F-sharp.

The upward and downward motions of the walking hand and arm also play a major role in intervals and chords. When we play single notes, a certain amount of weight is needed for the key to go down with ease. When playing an interval with two keys, twice as much weight is needed, and as more notes are added to a chord, proportionately more weight is necessary.

Forearm weight doesn't replace finger motion in any aspect of playing, including chord and interval playing. However, the most effective way to initially get the right amount of forearm weight behind the fingers for interval and chord playing is to first tell the student, "Let the forearm put down the keys." Initiating from the forearm in this way, the student begins to feel the right amount of weight needed for the fingers to put down the keys with ease. Coupled with control of key speed, this additional forearm weight not only makes it easy to put the keys down without the fingers having to push and press but also profoundly affects the volume and quality of sound. While the fingers play a lesser role in chord playing than in single note playing, there is still a sense of finger aliveness as they go down with the keys. In most cases, it's usually enough to feel the contact between the fingertips and the keys to obtain the proper balance between finger and arm activity.

Playing with more weight does not mean using all the weight at our disposal but instead only releasing the amount of weight necessary for the keys to go down with ease. Nor does playing with more weight mean landing low or relaxing the wrist. The hand, wrist, and forearm should land on the key at the correct height for them to always feel connected. When playing a chord, if there is not enough weight behind each finger of the chord, the keys tend to not go down together. They also feel heavy and the fingers often feel weak. As with everything else in this technique, one must learn to balance between two extremes. It is essential to remember that the released weight does not come from the upper arm. Instead, the upper arm stays in a position that enables the playing apparatus to move freely and correctly.

Combining walking hand and arm and rotation in interval and chord playing. In interval and chord playing, the rotation is always a double rotation in the direction of the thumb, since rotating to the fifth finger would throw the hand off balance. Although the rotation comes from the side, the landing is always straight down into the keys, with forearm weight equally distributed over all the playing fingers. Finally, moving from one interval or chord to another is done with a staccato touch. I discuss this point in the section on octaves.

Going from intervals or chords to single notes and back. When going from intervals or chords to single notes or from denser chords to less dense chords, the common tendency is to use more weight with the denser chord and not enough weight with the less dense chord or single note. This takes away from the feeling of solidity that comes from the arm being behind every single note and chord. A typical example occurs with slurs. The common pedagogical instruction is to play down on the chord and up on the less dense chord or single note, often with the wrist going down and up. However, this breaks the alignment between the hand and the forearm. Also, since the second note of the slur does not receive the necessary forearm support, it is often hardly heard, and the musical connection to what comes next is lost.

When this occurs, I suggest playing down on the first note or chord and then consciously playing down on the second note or chord. That will then integrate into the down-up shape of a slur. The same two consecutive down motions take place between all combinations of chords, intervals, and single notes in two-note slurs.

While chords and intervals require double rotation, combinations of chords and single notes require combinations of single and double rotation. In the example of moving from the interval G and B played with the third and fifth finger in the right hand to the C with the thumb, the rotation is to the left on the interval and left to the thumb: a double rotation. Similarly, descending from one interval to another is also a double rotation, such as going from G and B with the third and fifth finger to C and E with the second finger and the thumb. Going in the reverse direction is more complex. It begins with a single rotation to the left from the thumb side, which sends the arm across to the right, ready to play the third and fifth fingers. This is the lateral aspect of the walking hand and arm. Upon arrival, since all intervals and chords always play in the direction of the thumb, the fingers should not be tilted to the right but instead should play down with a slight rotational balance to the left. I call this complicated combination a *hybrid rotation* because it starts with a single rotation and ends with a double rotation. This allows equal forearm support behind each finger. This hybrid rotation can also occur when moving between intervals at a distance from each other, such as moving from C and E with the first and second fingers to G and B with the third and fifth fingers.

When an interval goes to a single note in an ascending passage, such as the thumb and second finger on C and E in the right hand going up to the fifth finger on A, the rotation from the interval to the single note is a single rotation. Going down, the rotation from a single note to an interval is a single rotation.

Note that rotation and walking hand and arm don't always move in the same direction. For example, in scales, the second, third, fourth, and fifth fingers move to the right as the walking hand and arm move to the right; however, in crossing to the thumb, the rotation of the thumb is to the left, in the opposite direction, while the forearm continues shifting to the right.

Rotation and walking hand and arm can only go so far without adding two more fundamental motions: in-and-out motions and shaping motions.

IN-AND-OUT MOTION

In-and-out motion refers to the movement of the entire arm from the fingers to the shoulder in toward the fallboard and out toward the body. It is initiated by the forearm, with the upper arm following. In-and-out motions are essential for three reasons:

1. They eliminate the twisting motions that occur when the thumb or the fifth finger (the two shortest fingers) have to play in the black key area, and the long fingers (the second, third, and fourth fingers) do not move into the black key area along with them. When the long fingers avoid playing in the black key area, the hand has to twist for the thumb or fifth finger to reach a black key. This twisting breaks the alignment between the hand and forearm as well as causing wrist pain and ganglia.

2. They prevent the long fingers from curling as they move out from the black to the white keys, as well as when they play in the white key area only.

3. They accommodate different finger lengths when going from a short finger to a long finger and back.

Pianists avoid playing in the black key area for two main reasons:

1. The keys feel heavier in the black key area than in the white key area because there is less leverage closer to the fallboard and as a result more weight is required to put the keys down.

2. The fingers feel either pulled apart from each other or crowded because the white keys are narrower in the black key area. Fingers may become stuck between black keys, causing them to go down unintentionally.

In-and-out motions solve both these problems. By themselves, the fingers don't have sufficient weight to overcome key heaviness. However, when they have the support and additional weight of the forearm as it moves in and out, they are then able to overcome the keys' weight. The feeling of heaviness disappears, and playing in the black key area feels as light as in the white key area. In-and-out motions also solve the problem of fingers feeling cramped in the black key area. Correct in-and-out motions combined with rotation position the fingers so that they fit more easily between the black keys.

In-and-out motions when moving between the white key and black key areas. When moving from the white key area to the black key area, the tendency is for the fingers to stay in the white key area until the last minute. This forces the hand to twist when the thumb arrives to play a black key. The way to avoid this twisting is for the arm to move in, bringing the fingers into the black key area as the thumb approaches the black key that it is going to play. With this help from the arm, the finger playing before the thumb arrives at the spot directly in front of where the thumb has to play next. The thumb can thus play without twisting. These motions should be small and gradual; if they are too sudden or large, they produce fatigue and pain in the shoulder and neck areas. A typical example that illustrates going from the white key area to the black key area is in the Bach D-minor Two-Part Invention for the right hand, when first the fifth finger and then the thumb have to play on a black key after the other fingers play on white keys. Returning to the white key area usually has to be done gradually as well.

In-and-out motions in the white key area. When we play scale-type passages in the white key area without in-and-out motions, one of the following negative scenarios occurs:

1. When moving from the thumb to any other finger the tendency is to curl the fingers in order to stay in the white key area. On the other hand, if the fingers retain their natural curve, the long fingers end up in the black key area, where the keys are heavier and the spaces narrower.

2. When going from the thumb to another finger, the hands have to twist in order to prevent the long fingers from being in the black key area.

These scenarios occur due to the erroneous assumption that it is the role of the fingers alone to move in and out to different key spots. Also, it is often taught that the thumb and the other four fingers must be in a straight line on the white keys, which immediately puts them in a curled position. Instead, the forearm brings the fingers to the right key location by moving in or out of the white key area. This enables the fingers to remain in their natural curved position at all times and eliminates curling and twisting.

In-and-out motions in the black key area. In-and-out motions in the black key area are just as important as in the white key area. They make it possible for the arm to balance over each finger, to overcome key heaviness, and to eliminate the feeling of being stuck while playing the narrow white keys within the black key area. Combined with rotation, in-and-out motions result in larger openings between the fingers than when they move sideways only. These larger openings between the fingers eliminate the feeling of the black keys pulling the fingers apart while playing on the white keys.

Timing in-and-out motions with rotation. The timing with which rotation and in-and-out motions merge is of great importance. The inward motion or outward motion must occur together with the second part of the rotation because if it occurs with the preparatory part of the rotation, the finger will have to curl or the hand will have to twist. Also, neither the finger that has just played nor the finger that is about to play should reach the destination by sliding. Instead, the forearm brings the fingers and hand close to the right key spot, where they can play straight down. This experience is the same as in walking: when walking either forward or backward, the foot doesn't slide to its destination. When this technique is properly learned and absorbed, so that each motion minimizes the other, there is very little sense of movement.

Forward-and-backward movement. Another form of in-and-out motion called forward-and-backward movement takes place where there is a minimal need to move. This motion is more of a forearm adjustment behind the playing finger than a change in the location of the finger on the key. An example of forward movement is when the short fifth finger plays G and the longer fourth finger is about to play F-sharp. Since the fourth finger is a longer finger, a simple forward motion of the forearm is all that is necessary to bring the forearm directly over it and give it support as it plays. An example of backward movement is when the fourth finger plays F-sharp and the fifth finger is about to play G. Since the fifth finger is shorter, it is already in the white key area and needs only a slight backward movement of the forearm to feel supported.

Combined with rotation and walking hand and arm, in-and-out motions give the playing apparatus the additional power necessary to overcome key resistance in both the white and black key areas and to produce a greater variety of sound.

SHAPING

Shaping, the fourth fundamental motion of the Taubman Approach, completes and minimizes the other motions. Its roundness makes playing feel easy and natural. Traditionally, the word *shaping* often means making circles with the arms, often as a way to relieve tension. These circles tend to be large and involve excessive motions of the upper arm and elbows. In some cases, shaping is initiated from the wrist. The term is also used to describe phrasing and the use of dynamics. In this chapter, I define what *shaping* means in the Taubman Approach.

In the Taubman Approach, shaping has both technical and interpretive aspects. As a physical phenomenon, shaping describes a round or elliptical rather than a flat or angular design. The forearm and hand move slightly higher and lower over a group of notes, creating curved and elliptical lines. This is done from the forearm, with small and gradual motions specific to the passage, resulting in greater efficiency, ease, naturalness, speed, and precision. When shaping is correctly applied, it combines with rotation, the walking hand and arm, and in-and-out motions, thus unifying, aligning, and helping to minimize them as well. Shaping brings all the basic movements under one umbrella and facilitates the playing, making it feel more natural and resulting in a musically shaped line rather than a static sound.

Shaping is not a wrist or upper arm motion. Shaping from the wrist breaks the alignment between the hand and the forearm, puts stress on the wrist by isolating it, and causes wrist pain. Shaping from the upper arm makes playing both slow and fatiguing. There are limits to how high and low the forearm and hand can go when shaping because if they move too high or too low, the alignment of the playing apparatus is broken. If the forearm is too high, there is a sense of holding it up and hovering. When the arm pulls away from the fingers, it cannot support them in key depression. Conversely, if the forearm is too low, its weight falls back off the keyboard in the direction of the body instead of being directly over the fingers. The wrist may collapse as well, causing the weight of the forearm to fall into it. This results in wrist pain, numbness, and tingling in the fingers.

How do we determine shaping? Shaping is determined by several elements:

1. the combination of long and short fingers
2. in-and-out motions
3. black and white key combinations
4. changes of direction
5. fingering combinations

OVERSHAPES AND UNDERSHAPES

Overshapes. An example of an overshape would be moving from five descending fingers in the right hand, going from B to A-sharp to G-sharp to F-sharp to E. Since the initial movement is from the short fifth finger on a white key to the longer fourth finger on the A-sharp key, the forearm moves slightly higher in order to give the fourth finger the full support it needs. As the fourth finger goes to the longer third finger, the forearm must again move slightly higher. As the third finger goes to the shorter second finger, the forearm now moves slightly lower. As the second finger goes to the thumb, the forearm must move slightly lower still. This entire sequence of movements forms a wave that we call an *overshape.* Playing these notes in the reverse direction is also an overshape. Going from shorter to longer fingers, however, is not always an overshape. The shape of each passage depends on its context: the notes that precede and follow that passage.

Undershapes. An example of an undershape is going from the thumb to the fifth finger on white keys. Ascending from C to D to E to F to G, the forearm initially moves slightly lower to the second finger and again lower to the third finger, and then slightly higher to the fourth and then the fifth finger, in a sequence of movements that forms a wave called an *undershape.*

General considerations:

1. Normally, only one shape works in any given passage. An exception is when playing five successive notes on white keys. Here, two possibilities of shaping exist because there are two different in-and-out motions.

2. Shaping corresponds precisely to the choreography of the passage.

3. Shaping takes place between notes as well as over long notes and rests.

4. Like all the other motions, shaping always occurs with the second part of the rotation.

5. The last note of each shape is the first note of the next shape.

6. Shaping continues without breaks throughout the piece.

7. As with the other fundamental motions, shaping functions best when used just enough to accomplish the task. Without it, the playing will feel awkward. Exaggerated shaping tends to erase other motions, and may replace finger motion as well. The correct shape gives a feeling of total comfort and security.

Calculating shapes. To feel the shape correctly, it is essential to understand its highest or lowest point. With overshapes, the high point is right in the middle of a group of notes. When the overshape is over an uneven number of notes, the high or low point is over the middle note, and when it is over an even number of notes, the high or low point is over the space between the two middle notes. For example, in a five note passage, the high or low point is over the third note. And in a four note passage, the high or low point is over the space between the second and third notes.

An exception to this rule is when crossing over to the thumb in an ascending scale or arpeggio in the right hand or in a descending scale or arpeggio in the left hand. In these cases, the high point is on the finger before the thumb crossing to make room for the thumb to cross. With undershapes, the low point of the shape is in the middle as well. One must be careful to ensure that the low point of the shape doesn't break the alignment.

Covering large distances requires greater rotation and walking hand and arm, but smaller and slightly flatter looking shaping, since excessive shaping makes it difficult for the forearm to move across to the next note without stretching. Chopin Etude Opus 10 No. 1 provides a good example of smaller shaping over large distances. When distances between the notes are small, such as in scale passages, the shaping movements are slightly more obvious. In other words, the proportions of the movements in relation to each other change according to the situation. When these different motions move as one combination, the amount of each motion in the mix depends on the needs of the passage.

Pedagogical insights about shaping. In teaching, we often introduce the different motions in sequence, because it is the best way for the brain and the hands to absorb them. Rotation is the first motion necessary to learn in order to align the fingers, hand, and forearm and thus to avoid finger isolation and stretching. The walking hand and arm and the in-and-out motions take less time, sometimes emerging naturally once all the parts involved work as one system. When shaping is added, all the movements begin to feel like one organism, and we use this unity when we approach new pieces. After learning each element separately and then combining, integrating, and minimizing them, we no longer need to break down the movements in every new piece. If there is a passage problem, we solve it and then incorporate the solution into the playing.

Once all the other motions have been learned and integrated, shaping often follows naturally since it is the most intuitive of all the fundamental movements. However, given the complexity and variety of shapes in music, intuition can only go so far. Without solid knowledge, it is easy to play the wrong shape, which causes technical problems. Fortunately, shaping can be learned and taught.

Another byproduct of shaping is that it profoundly affects musical interpretation. The higher and lower motions of shaping produce different combinations of weight and speed into the key, which give the pianist the ability to effortlessly and naturally produce an unlimited variety of dynamics and to control the sound of every note. Passages that previously sounded dull and emotionless suddenly come to life.

CHAPTER THREE VIDEO EXAMPLES

To view in-depth video examples for the topics covered in this chapter visit:

www.ednagolandsky.com/chapter-3

Or you can just hold most mobile device cameras over the QR code below and they will instantly pull up the webpage for you:

OTHER TECHNICAL ASPECTS

In addition to discovering the foundational movements that comprise a healthy piano technique, Dorothy Taubman also examined all the specific technical challenges that piano repertoire presents, and developed solutions to these challenges as well. In this chapter, I show how the Taubman Approach enables pianists to play octaves rapidly and without tension, how to leap large distances with security, how to group phrases for ease of playing, and the necessity for both hands to function interdependently for the best results.

OCTAVES

Playing octaves rapidly and without tension is an aspect of piano technique that has long been a mystery. We hear well-known pianists past and present play dizzyingly fast octaves and chords. Yet for many pianists and piano students, regardless of the many hours of practice, octave speed is not forthcoming and serious problems often ensue. This is because, as with all elements of piano technique, the eye sees only a fraction of the mechanism that makes octave playing rapid and reliable. With octaves, all that can be seen is the arm moving down, up, and across the keys. In this section, I show how the different elements of the technique enable easy, secure, and fast octave and chord playing. I discuss how to open the hand without stretching, the use of staccato touch, and hand, forearm, and knuckle positions in octave playing. Rotation in octaves is explained, followed by tone production, including the best fingering for octaves and how to make them sound legato. Finally, I discuss traditional practices in playing octaves, note potential pitfalls, and offer strategies for teaching octaves.

OPENING THE HAND

Opening the hand in octave playing without stretching is essential for keeping the hands healthy. This is the first step to avoiding tension, which prevents freedom and speed. Most piano students automatically assume that they need to stretch their hands in preparation for playing octaves, including pianists with hands large enough to comfortably reach a ninth or even a tenth. When I tell people to just open the hand comfortably without stretching, they are often surprised to see that their hand is big enough to cover an octave without needing to stretch.

When the hand stretches to its extreme range, the opposing closing muscles pull in the opposite direction since they are not meant to go that far. As a result, instead of becoming bigger, the hand span actually shrinks. Since many pianists with average-sized hands are able to play octaves without stretching and at great speed, Taubman thought that there had to be a way to open the hand without stretching.

Pianist and pedagogue Otto Ortmann stated in his *Physiological Mechanics of Piano Technique*: "When an outside agency assists in moving a part of the body, it relieves the burden of the muscles responsible" (1929, 78). To illustrate, let the right hand stay in its closed natural position and use the left hand, the "outside agency" in this case, to open it. When opened passively in this way, the right hand can be opened to its maximum capacity without tension, since muscle usage is minimal.

At the piano, one outside agency is the keys themselves, since they help to open the hand as the fingers play. Another outside agency is the free drop of the forearm, since that helps open the hand as well. For people with smaller hands, having the hand open passively is especially important. They usually need to play the octave closer to the edge of the white key. Although adults' hands don't grow, this passive opening allows the hands to open to their maximum size, making them feel larger.

Although the hand opens sideways, the direction of the playing fingers must be down into the keys and not away from each other, which is called splaying. Splaying uses both the abductor and flexor muscles simultaneously, and the antagonistic pulls that result lead to tension and pain.

Finally, for young children whose hands are not fully developed, if there is tension or strain when opening the hand properly, it is best to either avoid playing octaves or to play quick, broken octaves. No one should ever resort to stretching.

STACCATO TOUCH

Another elemental problem is thinking that octave playing requires actively moving the forearm up and down. Ortmann tested this hypothesis and concluded that this type of arm motion is not fast enough for quick octave playing (1929, 78). However, as Taubman pointed out, there are pianists who play octaves with breathtaking speed, which means that there has to be another way for the arm to go up and down rapidly without fatigue.

Taubman explained that instead of the forearm actively moving itself up and down, it can be sent up freely by an outside agency, which in this case is staccato touch, and comes down freely due to another outside agency: gravity. When done properly, this movement is quick and free of tension. The outside agencies of staccato touch and gravity allow octaves to be played with minimal muscular usage.

It is important to note that the upper arm is not actively involved in the up-and-down motions described above. These are done solely from the forearm, moving from the elbow fulcrum.

Staccato is generally understood as a finger action that gets the finger off the key as quickly as possible. Teachers frequently use the image of "hot keys" or "touching a hot stove" to emphasize the rapidity of this action. This imagery makes the fingers curl into the hand and results in extreme tension. It also stops the playing mechanism in midair, which necessitates either actively bringing the arm back down or taking the time to release the tense muscles and allow the forearm to fall down on its own. All of this reduces speed.

Another problem that traditional approaches have not taken into account is that the upward motion in staccato playing cannot occur without an initial downward motion, just like jumping on a trampoline or bouncing a ball. At the piano, upon reaching the keybed, which is the downward motion, a small fingertip action is sufficient to send the playing apparatus back up. This is followed by another continuous down-up combination as the fingers, hand, and forearm move to the next octave. This small finger action at the bottom of the key, which Taubman called a "fingertip pluck," is so small that it is virtually invisible to the naked eye, but it is powerful enough to send the fingers, hand, and forearm quickly up and across to the next octave without tension. With forearm support, this fingertip pluck is the mechanism for moving from octave to octave with minimal muscle usage and without curling.

The smallest staccato in existence is when we play repeated octaves and chords. The fingers should not leave the keys. The keys come up just enough to pass the point of sound before going down again. We call this "riding the keys up and down," and this minimal motion allows for great speed.

Legato sounding octaves. Legato sounding octaves are covered in the next chapter, in the section where I discuss how to produce legato sounds.

HAND, WRIST, FOREARM, AND KNUCKLE POSITIONS IN OCTAVE PLAYING

When the hand opens up to play octaves, the forearm and wrist automatically become higher, and the main knuckles become slightly flatter looking. While somewhat flatter, the top knuckles are not collapsed, so they can still act as the main fulcrum for finger action. Also, flattening the hand too much may lead to a relaxation of the bridge, breaking the connection between the fingers and the hand and resulting in a feeling of weakness, tension, and often backache. In contrast, if the knuckles are too high, the opening of the hand becomes limited. When the wrist and knuckles are in their correct positions, the hand feels solid and strong.

ROTATION IN OCTAVE PLAYING

The feeling of solidity mentioned above is also aided by rotation. As elsewhere, rotation speeds up octave playing. Like all other intervals and chords, octave rotations are always in the direction of the thumb, which makes them double rotations. Upon landing, the forearm has to be balanced equally behind both fingers rather than tilting toward the thumb, which would prevent the forearm from balancing and supporting both fingers equally. The traditional teaching of leading with the fifth finger in ascending octaves and leading with the thumb in descending octaves destroys this balance and should be avoided.

FINGERING

The best fingering for octave playing, regardless of whether the octaves are on white or black keys, is the thumb and the fifth finger. Pianists use the third or fourth finger in octave playing, hoping to achieve legato and increase speed. However, using these fingers causes stretching and twisting. In fact, using the third finger in this way can result in career-ending injuries. Pianists with large hands may use the fourth finger on black key octaves if there is no feeling of stretching or twisting and it seems as comfortable as when playing with the fifth finger. Yet when I show them how to get both speed and the effect of legato octaves with the fifth finger only, almost all of them prefer to use the fifth finger, since it is more comfortable and all the octaves feel uniform.

OTHER HARMFUL PRACTICES IN OCTAVE PLAYING

The tools outlined in the preceding section offer pianists the possibility of playing free and comfortable octaves. Unfortunately, many harmful practices exist that hamper easy octave playing.

When I was in the conservatory, I was told that curling the second finger would create additional firmness and security. However, curling not only causes tension but also makes the hand even smaller, which causes it to stretch even more. The second finger should never be used in this way.

Another common practice is to play octaves from the wrist. These "wrist octaves" are actually isolated hand motions from the wrist joint that usually go to the extreme range of motion, causing acute tension and pain in the wrist and forearm. In the same way that lack of understanding of the underlying mechanism of finger motion has led to isolated finger exercises, the lack of understanding of the underlying mechanism in octave and chord playing has led to these isolated hand motions and the exercises that accompany them. In both cases, the break in alignment causes inefficiency, tension, and pain. What the eye doesn't perceive in healthy, coordinated octaves are the tiny accompanying forearm motions. As in all other aspects of playing, the alignment of the fingers, hand, and forearm has to be maintained throughout in order to play octaves successfully.

As previously mentioned, the entire discussion of octaves is relevant to chord playing as well. With chords, however, special attention should be directed to the playing of the middle fingers, which often do not get enough forearm support. The amount of forearm support should be the same over each playing finger. As more notes are added to the chord, forearm support should increase proportionately.

The non-playing fingers (in octaves, the second, third, and fourth fingers) should rest lightly on the keys, since resting excessive weight on the keys takes weight away from the playing fingers. Pianists often hold the second, third, and fourth fingers up and away from the keys when playing octaves, out of fear that they will play extraneous notes. This causes dual antagonistic pulls, resulting in tension. When octaves are played correctly, the forearm's weight is directed only into the first and fifth fingers.

In chord playing, people tend to rebound more on the thumb and fifth fingers and less on the middle finger or fingers, with the result that speed suffers. All the fingers need to rebound equally.

When playing octaves on black keys, pianists tend to arch the thumb and flatten the fifth finger. The thumb and fifth finger should play the keys in the same way as when playing white key octaves.

Sometimes, as the hand and the forearm go up in the air, the hand and/or the fingers drop down, away from the forearm. This breaks the alignment between the fingers, hand, and forearm. The fingers must always remain in their natural curved position and move together with the hand and forearm.

TEACHING OCTAVES

When I teach octaves, I first cover the basic principles discussed above, such as opening the hand, finger, knuckle, and wrist positions, and the importance of using a staccato touch to avoid stretching. I then have the student play freely down into each octave, stopping on the key bottom. I check to make sure that the wrist and forearm are at the correct height. The student then plays an octave scale while feeling the proper landing on each octave with the support of the forearm for one week. If all goes well, the following week I introduce the word *rebound.* I explain that when the fingers reach the keybed, the rebound of the finger, hand, and forearm takes them as a unit to the next octave. If the rebound is too weak and doesn't create an automatic response, I suggest a small fingertip action at the keybed. It is impossible to see this small pluck that is taking place since it doesn't change the curved shape of the fingers. For greater efficiency and speed, I ask the student to minimize the upward motions by going directly from key surface to key surface. As mentioned earlier, the addition of rotation also increases speed.

When playing a slow and expressive line of octaves, remaining for the full duration of the notes as written and moving to the next octave at the last second results in playing too fast down into the next octave. A singing tone requires slowing down the key, so it is necessary to arrive at the next octave in time to control the speed of the fingers into the keys. This is immediately followed by a staccato touch that sends the playing apparatus to the next octave.

Once the student is able to produce a singing tone on a single octave, they then play the entire octave passage without stopping, controlling the sound of each octave. The ear informs us whether we are getting the intended results. We need to listen to ourselves objectively, just as we listen to other pianists. That information allows us to adjust weight and speed accordingly until we get the desired tone. The use of pedal further enhances the legato effect.

LEAPS

Piano music is filled with quick leaps of every size. Being able to play them rapidly, securely, and without getting tired is essential for a well-functioning technique.

A leap is made up of two notes: the note we are leaping from and the note we are leaping to. A common tendency is to focus so much on the second note of the leap that the first note does not get the necessary attention. As a result of ignoring the first note, the fingers tend to stretch and pull over to reach the second note, even though the distance between the notes is often greater than a hand span. This causes fatigue and tension, and reduces speed. Also, the pianist has to actively move the arm over to the second note, which makes the movement bigger, slower, and less accurate.

The importance of paying proper attention to the first note of the leap is essential for secure and accurate leaps. This is analogous to long jumping, where the athlete needs to come down strongly on the step before the jump in order to obtain the necessary force to make the jump. At the piano, we emphasize the first note of the leap for the same reason. However, this emphasis should not produce an unwanted accent.

LEGATO LEAPS

There are two types of leaps: legato leaps and staccato leaps. Legato leaps are essentially a larger version of the rotational motions that take place in scale-type passages. These quick rotational motions combine with the walking hand and arm to move across longer distances as well. The difference is that while a small preparatory rotation is sufficient to move the playing apparatus across smaller distances, a larger one is needed as the distance increases in order to prevent either stretching or actively moving the arm to get to the next key. We can compare it to throwing a ball. Throwing a ball begins by moving the arm back in the opposite direction; the greater the throwing distance, the farther back the arm moves. In the same way, at the piano the size of the preparatory motion needs to be proportionate to the distance of the leap.

During the preparatory motion, the finger on the first note should not push off or let go of the bottom of the key. From the preparatory motion to the end of the leap, as the forearm and hand move across the distance, the hand always remains in its natural unstretched position. The larger preparatory motion quickly sends the fingers, hand, and forearm to their destination. Like the ball that is being thrown, the forearm does not actively move itself during the leap but is sent by the preparatory motion. We control the preparatory motion and the landing but let the arm move freely in between. The result of these correct motions is that distances feel smaller and the piano seems to have shrunk in size.

The idea that moving in one direction requires a preparatory motion in the opposite direction may seem counterintuitive at first, but it works like magic. Instead of working for hours on leaps and feeling frustrated that the passage is still insecure, leaps become so natural that there is a sense that the arms have acquired a brain of their own.

As rotation and walking hand and arm move the playing apparatus quickly between the two notes of the leap, at some point the playing finger leaves the first note. The movement is so fast that it is not felt. Otherwise, if we consciously let go of that first note, the leap feels less secure. For leaps to be successful, our perception needs to be that of feeling legato.

STACCATO LEAPS

In situations where legato is not possible, a staccato rebound on the first note sends the finger hand and forearm powerfully and quickly across to the second note. It typically occurs over large distances with intervals or chords, when going from single notes to intervals or chords to single chords, or when one hand crosses over the other. The feeling is one of being sent automatically rather than that of initiating an active movement. Depending on the distance to be covered, staccato touch has slightly different speeds. If the distance is large, a shorter staccato is needed in order for the playing apparatus to be sent. If the distance is shorter, a staccato that is less short will suffice.

To attain maximum efficiency and speed, the upward motion should be as small as possible, just enough to allow the hand and forearm to move sideways across to the second note. Adding rotation further increases the speed of the leap and decreases the amount of forearm motion. The result is ease, security, consistency, and efficiency.

When practicing both legato and staccato leaps, it is helpful to pause right before the first note of the leap. This pause helps to emphasize the first note, thereby allowing the playing apparatus to be sent accurately to the second note. Once practiced that way and internalized, this pause no longer needs to be conscious.

OTHER FACTORS IN PLAYING LEAPS

1. Distances in leaps should be measured from the closest note. This gives a more realistic sense of the distance the arm must travel and shrinks the distance of the leap. For instance, when we play an octave with the thumb on middle C and the fifth finger on the next C and then leap one octave up, the thumb replaces the fifth finger on the C above middle C, which is the closest note.

2. In repeated leaps left and right, the elbow should be equidistant from the two notes. This keeps the upper arm relatively still and eliminates the sense of distance.

3. When simultaneous leaps occur in both hands and they are of different distances, the hand with the smaller distance moves first, since the brain can't concentrate on two activities at the same time. When the leaps are of the same or similar size, the left hand usually moves first. Upon arrival, they both play together. These movements happen so quickly that the eye can't see the distinction, but they make all the difference in organizing the leap and in feeling secure. In general, if both hands leap to the right, the right hand moves first, and if both hands leap to the left, the left hand moves first.

4. In leaps between intervals and chords, the rotation is always in the direction of the thumb, making it a double rotation. Leaping from a single note to an interval or chord can be either a single or a double rotation, depending on the context.

5. The upward motion in staccato leaps should be minimized and the

focus should be on lateral movement, which saves time. When first practicing the leap, the student may need to slightly exaggerate the upward motion to feel its freedom. Once the leap is mastered, the upward motion should be reduced.

GROUPING

Grouping is based on the fact that the brain can process only a limited amount of information at one time. According to psychologist George Miller, the brain can handle only five to nine "chunks" (elements) of information at a time (1994). However, when information is divided into small groups, the brain can hold larger amounts. For example, sentences are intelligible because of punctuation, and phone numbers are more easily remembered due to the spaces between groups of numbers.

At the piano, *grouping* refers to organizing notes into groups. Phrases often consist of complex designs that can make the playing feel disorganized, difficult, or awkward. Grouping organizes the phrase into smaller clusters of notes by putting minuscule spaces between them. This organization makes the phrase easier to play. Although the pianist thinks and feels these spaces, they are not obvious enough to be heard by the listener and do not affect the overall continuity of the phrase. Once the pianist practices and learns the phrase in this way, the hand plays it automatically and they are free to concentrate on the music.

At times grouping involves physical breaks between the groups, while at other times it occurs while playing legato. In both cases, rotation, walking hand and arm, in-and-out motions, and shaping continue from the last note of one group to the first note of the next group; if not, the fluidity, evenness, and comfort of the overall passage suffer. Finally, the first note of each new group is not accented unless an accent is desired musically.

In the following section, I discuss different categories of grouping, such as changes of direction to the musical line, different densities of notes, grouping to avoid stretching, dealing with complex metric designs, and long passages of running notes.

DIFFERENT CATEGORIES OF GROUPING

Changes of direction. In passages that go up and down the keyboard, changes of direction without grouping can be confusing and fatiguing. In this case, notes are grouped starting at the beginning of each change of direction. For example, when there is a scale passage up the keyboard followed by a leap downward and then another scale passage upward, grouping is organized according to the dominant direction, which is the ascending group of notes. Conversely, if the scale passage goes down the keyboard and is followed by an upward leap, the dominant direction is the descending group of notes. Grouping is also used to organize passages that go in and out of the black key area in the same way. To avoid confusion, one direction always needs to be dominant.

Different densities of notes. When a passage contains combinations of intervals and single notes, or chords going to intervals or single notes, grouping generally starts with the denser clusters. Since more weight is required to play the interval or chord, it is necessary for the forearm to settle its weight behind the playing fingers. Starting the group from the denser cluster makes it easier for the forearm to do this. There are exceptions to the above guideline. If grouping from the denser to the less dense cluster or single note causes stretching, it is advisable to group from the less dense cluster or single note to the denser cluster. When unsure, one can try both approaches and choose the one that feels easier.

Grouping to avoid stretching. We group notes that are close to each other so that the hand feels only these small, easy groups. Even when we physically disconnect between groups, all the other basic motions still act to move from the last note of one group to the first note of the next group. Another benefit of this kind of grouping is that it creates a sense of uniformity in the hands, avoiding the feeling of the hand opening and closing.

Grouping in complex metric designs. Taubman's basic principle states that "in speed we cannot go to and from a quick note, only from a quick note." For example, when dotted eighth notes are going to sixteenth notes, the hand has to get off the long note quickly and wait on the quick note. This applies to any situation where we have alternating long and short durations of sound.

If we follow the traditional thinking of holding the long notes down to their full written value, we arrive too late to play the quick note in time, especially in rapid passages. Pianists often linger too long on the long note because they want a legato effect. This creates insecurity, leads to inaccuracy, and limits the ability to control the sound of the quick notes. The solution is to get off the long note using a staccato touch while keeping the sound going with the pedal, and quickly get to the short note to start the next grouping from there. With the right tonal control, there is time to express both the long and the short notes, matching the two sounds to create a musical line. Quickly getting off the long note is another example of an aspect of technique that is counterintuitive yet nevertheless essential to attain the right technical and musical results.

Grouping long-running passages. There are passages that do not have a clearly delineated grouping. Mozart and Haydn sonatas or concerti contain many passages with running sixteenth notes. Without grouping them, the pianist can experience a sense of confusion and lack of control. In these cases, notes should be organized according to the beat, in groups of four, six, eight, and occasionally nine notes. The fresh start and the sense that we are only responsible for the notes within a group facilitates the playing. Adding emphasis to the first note of each group gives it extra impetus to move forward and eliminates the feeling of being out of control. This does not mean accenting the beginning of each group or waiting between the groups. Instead, what is felt and heard is smoothness with no sense of rushing, and the time to express one's thoughts and wishes through the music.

INTERDEPENDENCE OF THE HANDS

Coordinating the hands is an important tool, not only for playing securely, but also for learning, sight-reading, and memorizing a piece of music. The most common way pianists learn a piece is to first practice with the hands separately, in the belief that this will enable them to play better when they put the hands together. Yet for many the result is the opposite. In spite of practicing every note of the piece in each hand, they continue to feel insecure and struggle to integrate the hands.

The reason for this insecurity and effort is that the brain can't concentrate fully on two different activities at the same time. According to pediatrics professor Dimitri Christakis, director of the Center for Child Health, Behavior and Development at Seattle Children's Research Institute, "The truth is you don't really multitask, you just think you do; the brain can't process two high-level cognitive things . . . What you are actually doing, is oscillating between the two" (Klass 2009). Many years ago, Dorothy Taubman expressed this same idea in relation to piano playing:

> When you learn one hand, you have learned one specific piece. When you learn the other hand, you have learned another totally different piece with a totally different set of reflexes and timing. Two different pieces are recorded in the mind, and after this is ingrained, you are expected to put them together and play a third way, just like that.

Accordingly, practicing with the hands together is of supreme importance.

Another problem with learning a piece with the hands separately is that the eye gets used to focusing on one line at a time, usually the right hand. As a result, when the hands play together, they don't get equal attention. This causes problems in both sight-reading and memorization. We often have memory slips in the "easy" hand, most often the left. In order to achieve real mastery of a passage or piece, both hands must consciously practice and learn it at the same time.

These problems arise from the failure to distinguish between the initial process of making changes in the basic technique, where it is necessary to work with the hands separately, and the subsequent process of learning a piece. When people first come with technical problems or injuries, we need to work with the hands separately in order to solve them. The pianist also learns the basic steps of rotation and scale crossing with the hands separately. As soon as rotation is minimized and integrated with the other motions, the student should begin to play with hands together and continue to learn new pieces with the hands together from then on. When a problem occurs in a specific passage, such as a fingering issue or an incorrect or missing motion, practicing can be done with the hands separately. However, as soon as the problem is resolved, the hands should return to playing together.

A piece of music is one cohesive piece divided by two hands, in the same way that a piece of chamber or orchestral music is one cohesive piece shared by a number of instruments. When learning a piece of music with the hands playing together, the pianist consciously integrates the two hands to create one entity and the two hands become unified, both technically and musically. As we begin to practice with the hands together and understand how they function interdependently, sight-reading and memorization improve. Also, in this way, the hands learn how to simultaneously play dissimilar types of passages.

Interdependence assists with vertical motions, horizontal motions such as rotation, in-and-out, and shaping. In addition, it solves problems that occur in passages with alternating hands, layering different tonal lines, troubleshooting polyrhythms, and strategies for legato versus staccato playing in different hands.

VERTICAL MOTIONS

Music moves horizontally from note to note, so it's easy to miss the fact that there is a vertical component as well. When both hands are playing simultaneously, they have to feel as if they are playing a chord. This is the most basic aspect of interdependence. At the piano we experience the tactile sense of the fingers putting down the keys at the same time with both hands. Once absorbed, this vertical experience frees us to concentrate on horizontal movements with much greater security.

HORIZONTAL MOTIONS

The horizontal movements between keys, such as rotation, walking hand and arm, in-and-out motions, and shaping, must all be interdependent, whether they are the same or different in the two hands.

Rotation. Identical movements that take place in both hands at the same time have to be felt simultaneously. This can be when both hands are playing single rotations, either going in the same direction or in opposite directions. When the motions are not identical, it is even more important for them to be felt simultaneously. An example of different movements taking place at the same time is when one hand has single rotations, such as a trill or an Alberti bass, while the other hand plays a scale containing both single and double rotations.

In-and-out motions. The pianist must be aware when his or her hands are moving in or out in the same direction. This is even more critical when the hands move in opposite directions.

Shaping. It is necessary to consciously feel when both hands have either the same or different shapes.

Over the years I have observed that there is a tendency for one hand to copy the other. As a result, when the two hands have different motions, one hand will end up playing incorrectly. For example, double rotations in one hand may not be completed when the other hand has only single rotations.

This tendency for one hand to copy the other also applies to both in-and-out and shaping motions. Unless this is corrected, these incorrect motions will lead to confusion and technical problems.

Another form of this copying problem is when the two hands are moving simultaneously but one hand has to move a greater distance than the other. The hand that has to move the greater distance may move too little, or the other hand may move too much. Both hands need to feel the appropriate amount of motion for their distance simultaneously. I call this aspect of interdependence "feeling the more against the less."

ALTERNATING HANDS

When there is a rapid passage with alternating hands, one hand has to cue or trigger the other as they go back and forth in a zigzag pattern. In fast playing, there is no time for each hand to know when to play unless one hand cues the other. Once the hands have mastered this pattern, it is enough to organize the playing in one direction, either from the left hand to the right hand or from the right hand to the left hand, depending on the passage. The hand that starts the passage is the one that usually determines this organization. Without interdependence training, the hands tend to collide and play together rather than alternating, and no amount of practicing with the hands separately can cure this problem.

Finally, in passages where one hand plays several notes and then the other hand continues, the last note of one hand cues the first note of the other.

INTERDEPENDENCE OF ORNAMENTS

Many ornaments are indicated with abbreviations or symbols (e.g., *tr.* for *trill*) or written in a smaller font. In addition, the notes themselves must often be played quickly. As a result, they are often considered less important than the other notes of the piece. However, the composer wrote them in order for them to be played and expressed, and since they are generally quick, the correct technique is especially important. In addition, they need to fit precisely together with the notes being played in the other hand.

INTERDEPENDENCE OF TONAL QUALITY AND VOLUME

I have often noted that pianists tend to bring out the main line and keep the secondary line or lines soft so that they don't overpower the main line. People often think that secondary lines are not important enough to express, not realizing that without them the piece becomes essentially a one-line piece. The interrelationship between the various lines is what makes a great piece of music. In order to accomplish this, the pianist needs to develop the technical control to express all these different lines as the composer indicated. The quality and volume of the different sounds must be balanced vertically so that even the softest sounds can be heard. The technique to control different tonal qualities and volume is explained in the next chapter.

When we play both hands together simultaneously, we bring the different sounds of each note in that formation into their appropriate balance. This is the learning phase of interdependence for color (the word that describes different qualities and volumes of sound). Once this is accomplished, we have the freedom to concentrate on the horizontal motion of the music. This makes for a full and rich performance where every line is heard clearly, the way it sounds in the playing of many great artists. One of the great contributions of the Taubman Approach is that it explains how to accomplish this fundamental physical skill and to always have control over sound quality and volume. In my video recording "The Forgotten Lines," I describe how balancing the various voices that occur simultaneously in music makes it possible to fully express what the composer wrote (2006).

Contrapuntal music, such as the Bach fugues, poses a special challenge. Learning these pieces should start with analyzing and playing the different voices, imitations, episodic material between the voices, and the dynamics and character of each line. The next step is to interrelate the two hands in the way discussed above. Once the proper vertical interrelation of color has been learned, it becomes automatic and allows us to concentrate on and express the horizontal lines. Like all other aspects of technique and musical expression, it becomes a skill that does not need to be learned with each subsequent piece of music.

POLYRHYTHMS

Polyrhythms are different rhythmic patterns played together simultaneously, such as two notes against three or three notes against four. The composer writes these polyrhythms with the intent of creating a unique effect. Each hand must play its notes evenly throughout the measure to create this effect, so the notes in the rhythmic pattern with fewer notes must fit precisely into the notes and spaces of the rhythmic pattern with more notes.

However, pianists can't always rely on fitting the fewer notes accurately into the line with more notes. They hope the hands will come in at the right time, or add pedal and use rubato to hide inaccuracies. This approach causes insecurity that only worsens with long strings of polyrhythmic figures, and endless practice doesn't solve the problem. To make it easier, some editions divide the passages with more notes into smaller groups, so that the two hands can fit together at certain points in the pattern and play in unison. However, this does not solve the problem either.

Instead, when the composer indicates the number of notes for each hand in a passage, the first step is to calculate the placement of the pattern with fewer notes arithmetically. For example, in measure 31 of Chopin's Nocturne Opus 9 No. 3, where eight notes are played in the right hand against three in the left hand, the space occupied by one note in the left hand equals two and two-thirds spaces in the right hand. After the first note of each pattern, which is played in unison, the next two notes are played by the right hand. Then the note in the left hand plays right before the fourth note in the right hand. Next come two more notes in the right hand, followed by one more in the left hand slightly after the sixth note, and the last two notes in the right hand finish the measure.

Since these notes cannot be played at the same time, one hand must cue the other, especially in rapid passages, to ensure rhythmic precision and technical security. There is a physical sensation of one finger triggering the other. Once worked in, this strong physical sensation goes beyond the thinking phase and we are free to concentrate on the music. In this example, the third note of the octuplet cues the second note of the triplet, and the sixth note of the octuplet cues the third note of the triplet, and this pattern repeats for the duration of the passage.

LEGATO AND STACCATO PLAYING

When one hand plays legato and the other hand plays staccato, both hands start by playing down into the key. However, the hand playing legato stays down while the staccato hand plays up. The movement up should not be excessive, so that the hand can remain close to the keys. This way the hands learn to experience both kinds of touch at the same time.

SIMULTANEOUS LEAPS

As discussed in the section on leaps, when both hands leap at the same time, the brain can only focus on one of them; as a result, one hand must be quicker than the other. The shorter leap is generally the quicker one because the distance is smaller. Both hands start and land together, but during the leap the brain first concentrates on the shorter leap and then shifts its attention to the larger leap. This all happens so quickly that it is imperceptible to an observer, but with this organization, the pianist feels control and security.

This shift of attention applies to staccato and legato leaps alike. However, when both hands are leaping in the same direction, for example to the right, the right hand will move first, and when both hands move to the left, the left hand moves first. This is to prevent the hands from colliding. The only exception to this rule is when the hands cross over each other.

Like other elements of correct technique, once the necessary aspects of interdependent playing are correctly practiced and absorbed and can be played automatically at speed, the pianist is free to concentrate on the music.

INTERDEPENDENT LISTENING

Interdependence training not only helped me with my playing, but also made me a better listener. I realized that previously I was focusing my attention mostly on the primary melody lines. After I began practicing interdependently, I noticed that I was listening to music more deeply and inclusively. I felt that I could hear every detail of the piece, just as the composer intended it to be heard.

FINGERING

Good fingering is an essential consideration as soon as we start learning a piece of music. Awkward fingering leads to awkward playing, and this can result in technical problems that no amount of practice can overcome. In contrast, good fingering gets absorbed quickly, and the hands do not forget it. It assures the minimum amount of motion, avoids twisting and stretching, and facilitates the laws of alignment and coordination that make playing easy and natural.

One should not follow the fingering in any given edition blindly. While notes, rhythm, and certain slurred indications should be followed diligently, fingering notation is not sacred. If fingering recommended in the score is awkward, uncomfortable, or causes tension and pain, then it should be replaced with more comfortable fingering.

When deciding on fingering, several factors must be taken into consideration:

1. It is preferable to stay in the white key area whenever possible, since the keys are lighter there. To do this, the thumb and fifth fingers play on the white keys and the second, third, and fourth fingers play on the black keys. This is illustrated in the sequence E, F-sharp, G-sharp, A-sharp, B in the right hand.

2. If staying in the white key area causes stretching, then fingering that uses the first and fifth fingers should play in the black key area.

3. The pianist should avoid stretching by selecting fingerings that use the widest part of the hand. This is accomplished by using the thumb in conjunction with another finger whenever possible.

4. When possible, fingering should be arranged to avoid the crowding of fingers over small distances.

5. Fingering that results in twisting should never be used.

6. Whenever possible, one should divide the passage between the hands in order to avoid stretching.

7. When hands are crossed over as notated on the page, the pianist should consider uncrossing them if it makes the passage easier and/or more playable.

8. The tradition of always ending a passage on the fifth finger or starting a passage with the thumb can at times make a passage more difficult and awkward. Ending on the fifth finger should not be the determining factor when deciding on the fingering.

9. Many passages appear to be identical and as a result invite pianists to use the same fingering. However, slight differences, such as in

distances between keys or changes in combinations of white and black keys, may make using the same fingering awkward. In these cases, the fingering should not remain the same but should change in accord with these differences.

10. One set of fingering usually suits most hands. However, fingerings might change due to smaller hand opening size and smaller spaces between fingers.

CHAPTER FOUR
VIDEO EXAMPLES

To view in-depth video examples for the topics covered in this chapter visit:

www.ednagolandsky.com/chapter-4

Or you can just hold most mobile device cameras over the QR code below and they will instantly pull up the webpage for you:

CONNECTING TECHNIQUE TO MUSICAL EXPRESSION

THE INTERSECTION OF CRAFT AND ART

Brahms wrote, "Without craftsmanship, inspiration is a mere reed shaken in the wind" (Degler 1976, 143). Up to this point, I have been explaining the basic building blocks that constitute the technical craft of piano playing. However, piano technique is not complete without including musical expression, which is also a part of the technical craft of piano playing. The Taubman Approach is unique in that it teaches the specific physical elements that underpin musical expression: tone production, shaping, legato, pedaling, and rhythm.

TONE PRODUCTION

The first step is to be able to produce tone of every quality and volume. A rich tone is the most sought-after and challenging aspect of tone production. The two basic elements of tone production are weight and speed into the key.

WEIGHT

Noted pedagogues such as Walter Gieseking, Gyorgy Sandor, Seymour Fink, and Lillie Philipp realized that fingers alone were not the answer to producing bigger sounds and that more weight was needed (Gieseking 1972, Sandor 1981, Fink 1992, Lillie 1982). They turned to the upper arm as the main source for this additional weight. However, as previously explained, the excessive weight of the upper arm makes it difficult for the fingers to move. Also, the slow muscles of the upper arm are not capable of moving quickly across the keyboard. Yet we hear pianists who play with great speed and a lush sound as well. Whether consciously or not, they are clearly doing something different.

Since fingers have little weight, when they move by themselves the resulting sound is thin. To increase volume, we are often told to go faster and harder into the keys. However, this results in a harsh percussive tone and leads to fatigue, tension, and bruised fingertips.

Using forearm weight instead of the weight of the upper arm solves both these problems. The forearm can move quickly and easily in all directions. In addition, it provides the weight necessary to produce tone of every kind. With forearm weight, the sound becomes thick and warm. The fingers no longer need to push on the key bottom, so the physical feeling improves as well. The added forearm weight makes all the difference.

A common misconception about tone production is that dropping weight into the key creates a shock, and that dropping the wrist is a good way to absorb that shock. However, if the weight drops into the wrist, the break in the alignment between the hand and forearm prevents the forearm weight from getting to the fingers and supporting them in key descent and tonal control. Also, weight falling into the wrist is the main cause of carpal tunnel syndrome. As mentioned previously, any break in alignment is detrimental to a healthy technique, so dropping the weight into the wrist can never be a solution to any technical problem, including tone production. There should never be a shock if the wrist is at the proper height and the finger lands correctly on the key bottom.

SPEED INTO THE KEY

The other essential element in tone production is key speed. As discussed earlier, the key can go down with minutely different speeds. As we slow down the key descent, sound decreases, which is how we get soft sounds, but when the key goes down too slowly, sound disappears. To avoid unwanted loud sounds, pianists tend to hold their arms and shoulders up, causing arm fatigue and insecurity.

To develop control over the speed of key descent, it helps to keep the fingers close to the key surface with the forearm resting behind them. The slowing down of the key to produce tonal qualities is very slight and has no effect on the sideways speed from key to key, which is determined by rotation combined with the walking hand and arm.

By researching and understanding the capabilities of the playing apparatus, the instrument, and how they combine, Taubman solved the riddle of tone production. To avoid loud and percussive sounds, the key has to be played slightly slower, and to compensate for the softer sound that results, additional weight from the forearm has to be added. This combination of slower key speed and additional forearm weight produces a bigger and rounder sound. The correct proportion of weight and speed into the key gives the control to produce all other sounds as well.

Slowing down the key and controlling the amount of weight are new and unfamiliar experiences for most pianists. Like all elements of technique, they don't occur at either extreme of the spectrum but somewhere in the midrange. The fingers should neither go too quickly nor too slowly into the key, nor should there be too much or too little weight, but always just the right amount from the forearm to get the job done. The ear is the final arbiter and the only body part that can inform us if we are getting the desired result.

Another gratifying byproduct of slowing down the key with weight instead of pushing and forcing on the key bottom is that it makes the fingertips feel cushiony and thick even when one's fingertips are not well padded. This comes from using the correct technique for tone production rather than being born with thick finger pads, as some people think.

Reading about tone production is very different from experiencing it, which generally occurs in a lesson under the guidance of a skilled Taubman teacher. The release of different amounts of weight with the help of gravity is invisible and minute, and the concept of slowing down key descent can seem mysterious until it is felt and practiced.

In the final analysis, it is the interaction of the playing apparatus with the key that is the sole determinant of the quantity and quality of sound. While we can feel music in our hearts and bodies, listen with our ears, and desire certain effects with our minds, those parts don't directly play or control the keys. By focusing on these minute changes of forearm weight and speed into the key, the Taubman body of knowledge enables the pianist to produce the desired tone at any time, regardless of how they feel on any given day and without having to be inspired to get the best possible sound from the piano.

LEGATO

The word *legato* refers to the connection of sounds. There is an assumption that legato connection can only be accomplished by physically connecting the notes of the line. When playing scale passages and other passages with smaller distances where finger connection is easy, physical legato is possible and, in fact, preferable.

However, legato lines often extend over large distances where physical connection is not possible, and trying to physically connect these notes causes stretching or twisting. An example of a case where physical connection is impossible is when playing a note in a melodic line followed by notes in a secondary line a long distance away. The finger has to disconnect from the melody note to move to the notes of the secondary line, and may have to disconnect again to return to the original melodic line. How can the long notes in the melody sound legato when we can't physically connect them?

It is essential to distinguish between the composer's intention and the process that gets us to the final result. Although the composer wants notes to be connected in sound, nowhere do they insist that these notes have to be connected physically. It is astounding to realize how many unconnectable distances between notes exist in musical scores. Nevertheless, our field emphasizes the physical connection of notes; to do otherwise is looked upon as cheating. Many pianists follow the dictum that "you don't change what the composer writes, on pain of death—even if it does hurt" (Montparker 1986, 13). As a result, we often think that what the music looks like on the page and what we need to do physically are one and the same. This has led to many problems, including serious injuries. Taubman called this way of thinking "enslavement to notation."

Legato has to go beyond this limited definition of finger connection. The problem of how to link notes to each other so they sound legato even if they are not physically connected is addressed through tone production (already discussed), pedaling, and physical shaping.

PEDALING

Pedaling is a crucial tool for connecting sounds. Pianists often use the pedal to cover up inconsistencies and unevenness, especially in scale passages, which results in blurred and uneven sounds. Ironically, pianists use the pedal when playing small distances such as scale passages where it is unnecessary, but often fail to use it in larger distances where it is impossible to physically connect the notes.

In addition to connecting notes, the pedal also enhances sound. When a key is held down, the damper lifts and allows the string or strings belonging to that key to vibrate. However, when the pedal is used, the dampers on all the piano keys lift, and this results in a much richer tone. To be clear, pedaling doesn't create a rich sound by itself, but only enhances what is already there. A weak or harsh sound will not turn instantly into a lush sound. We need control over both tone production and the pedal in order to keep the sound rich and continuous when the fingers cannot physically connect.

PHYSICAL SHAPING

In the section on shaping, I explained the powerful role of shaping as a foundational movement in a natural technique. I also mentioned how shaping changes the music from sounding static to sounding round. Physical shaping is also essential to link sounds, whether or not they are physically connected. As the forearm moves higher and lower over a group of notes, it creates curved lines and a continuity of sound that enhances legato effect. Conversely, in the example of playing five consecutive adjacent notes, playing without shaping sounds "notey" even though the notes are physically connected. Shaping is essential to creating a legato effect whether the notes are connected or not.

When combined with tone production and pedaling, physical shaping produces another remarkable benefit. As these skills work together, they make it possible to time rubato so that it sounds compelling rather than exaggerated or artificial. Tone, shaping, and pedaling offer various possibilities of timing within phrases, between phrases, and over long notes and rests.

PRODUCING LEGATO-SOUNDING OCTAVES

Producing a legato-sounding line when playing octaves is almost inconceivable to most pianists. Nevertheless, the techniques previously outlined in this chapter enable pianists to produce this legato effect with octaves and chords as well as with single-note passages. Legato-sounding octaves are played with the staccato touch, just like regular octaves. A rich legato effect in staccato octaves can be achieved by using tonal control, pedaling, and shaping, without having to resort to twisting or stretching. Pressing on the fifth finger is often recommended in order to bring out the melody in octaves and chords, but can result in pain and injury to the finger. Knowing how to produce tone properly solves this problem.

In summary, the Taubman Approach offers a greatly expanded view of legato that goes beyond the idea of physical connection. Along with tone production, it helps to free us to translate our ideas into our playing and offers physical tools to realize our musical intentions.

RHYTHM

Any discussion of musical expression would be incomplete without the addition of the essential element of rhythm. In working with pianists, I noticed that even when they had acquired a good technique, were able to produce different qualities of sound and control of volume, and played with great expressivity, their playing at times lacked a sense of aliveness, excitement, and forward motion. I realized that what was missing was a stronger sense of pulse, but when I asked them to add it, their response was to either drop their wrist on the downbeats, play with unwanted accents, make the pulse so soft that it could not be heard, or ignore it altogether. I knew then that I didn't have the specific tools to teach this stronger sense of pulse so that it would project effectively to the listener. Accordingly, I embarked on learning more about rhythm and finding and implementing the most effective ways to teach it.

The results of my investigations were eye-opening and exciting. I realized that just as in the technical sphere, where several motions combine together to form one organism, the same happens on the expressive side: rhythm combines with and depends on tone production and shaping. Adding a pulse makes the musical result so much more compelling. These discoveries led me to call a set of videos that I taped on the subject "The Art of Rhythmic Expression" (2004). Another unexpected insight was that the correct handling of the beat helped the technique as well, organizing it in a way that made the playing physically easier and helped the music move forward without rushing. Regardless of whether the music was fast or slow, there was always a sense of a natural motion forward.

Rhythm is one of the basic elements in music that people respond to regardless of background and knowledge. It is one of the ways in which music speaks to us as a universal language. The pulse in music echoes the heart, the rhythm of life, as well as our surroundings. Much classical music is based on popular songs and dances of the day, as well as galloping horses, bells ringing, birds chirping, and other elements of daily life. It reflects the life and the world in which composers lived. The energy and immediacy that inspired great composers carried over to the pieces they wrote, and it should be carried over to the way we perform them.

Some people may think of rhythm simply as a durational pattern. Christopher Hasty, a professor at Harvard University, argues against such a narrow definition. Instead, he attempts to "return the word 'rhythm' to a central place in music where it can affirm the value of a kinesthetic, ongoing, open (i.e., present) involvement that would unite form and performance" (1999, 280). As Swiss educator Emile Jaques-Dalcroze puts it, "rhythm is motion," and in music, rhythm is the element that is "the most closely related to life" (1965, 40, 57).

According to Meredith Little and Natalie Jenne, in *Dance and the Music of Johann Sebastian Bach*, "Rhythm, according to the ancient Greek writer Aristoxenus, is an activity, not a thing. In earlier times the word rhythm was used as a verb—'I will rhythm these notes or I will rhythm these harmonies.' Thus, to rhythm something was to give it an organization, a shape, a form, and a distinctive life" (2001, 16).

DEFINITIONS OF THE BEAT

A discussion of rhythm and rhythmic motion is impossible without defining the beat that generates it, as well as the general sense of meter. I believe that one of the main reasons that people often find classical music inaccessible and boring is due to the fact that it does not always exude the energy and excitement that comes with correct handling of the beat.

The *Harvard Dictionary of Music* defines the beat as the temporal unit of the composition. It says that in moderate tempo, the 4/4 measure includes four beats, the first and third of which are strong, and the others weak. The 3/4 measure has three beats, only the first of which is strong. In quick tempi there may be two beats or even only one beat to the measure. In contrast, in very slow tempi, the beats may be felt in subdivisions of the main beat (Randel 1978, 45).

In life, it is the beating of our heart that keeps us alive. If it stops long enough, we die. Our own individual pulse responds to changes in our world—speeding up when in danger, slowing down when relaxed—to match the rhythm of our own life. It is the same with a piece of music: each piece has a distinct beat that helps define its unique character and mood. When the rhythmic feeling of the beat combines with tone production and shaping, the result is what I call a *musical beat.*

As we know, jazz has its own way of dealing with the beat and its subdivisions, which results in that wonderful and exciting rhythmicality. As Duke Ellington famously said, "It don't mean a thing if it ain't got that swing" (1932). And in the words of Wynton Marsalis, jazz trumpeter and director of Jazz at Lincoln Center, swing is "willful participation with style and groove" (2001).

THE SO-CALLED WEAK SECOND BEAT

In addition to expressing the strong beats in a measure, the other beats must be expressed as well. Every beat should be alive and accounted for, but not necessarily played in the same way. To my way of thinking, there are no weak beats, simply differently expressed beats. The word "weak" can be misleading because it implies that a "weak" beat is not important. However, in many instances, the second beat in a measure becomes a strong beat that needs to be expressed, as in a sarabande or a mazurka. Beyond that, a strong second beat and even a strong fourth beat occur routinely throughout the musical repertoire, whenever a composer wants to create syncopation. In short, if any beat is overlooked, the forward motion of the music suffers. For this reason, I prefer to call these beats "less strong" rather than "weak." The continuing pulsation should also be felt during rests and long notes.

COMBINING RHYTHM WITH TONE PRODUCTION AND SHAPING

Like the other aspects of technique, tone production and shaping play a central role in rhythmic expression. A small release of forearm weight, minutely greater than that used to produce a singing tone, combines with an almost imperceptible delay in playing the note to give the beat greater emphasis. The amount of weight and delay vary from piece to piece and even from phrase to phrase, depending on the musical intention.

Shaping is the motion that makes it possible to define strong and less strong beats. As the forearm moves higher and lower over a group of notes it allows the beats to be expressed differently, depending on where they occur in the arc of the shape. A typical example can be seen in the left-hand pattern of a waltz, where the first beat is played down, and the second and the third notes are played up. Without shaping, all notes would be played the same. Playing this way makes the music sound static and unmusical, and doesn't propel it forward.

CONCLUSION

In combination with tone production and shaping, rhythm helps define the character of a musical piece. Even more, it is the unique element in music that invites listener participation. Toe tapping, foot stomping, clapping, singing, and dancing are all results of the beat in music. While the beat in classical music may not be as obvious as in other musical genres, it still has an essential role in communicating the essence of the music to the listener. If the pianist can identify the rhythmic patterns of the piece and bring out both the strong and less strong beats in their appropriate manner, his or her connection to both the music and the audience will be more fulfilling, and the audience experience will be more rewarding as well.

CHAPTER FIVE
VIDEO EXAMPLES

To view in-depth video examples for the topics covered in this chapter visit:

www.ednagolandsky.com/chapter-5

Or you can just hold most mobile device cameras over the QR code below and they will instantly pull up the webpage for you:

TAUBMAN APPROACH PEDAGOGY

FACTORS IN THE TAUBMAN APPROACH LEARNING PROCESS

From my long pedagogical experience, I have observed several significant factors that affect how well and how quickly a student learns. In this chapter I cover different categories of students, with varying abilities and attitudes. How effectively one practices is crucial, as well as the frequency of lessons, especially at the beginning. I discuss the obstacles that students encounter in learning this work, share pedagogical insights from my own experience in teaching the Approach over many years, and end with a description of the process of becoming a Taubman teacher.

DIFFERENT TYPES OF STUDENTS

The ideal is for the student to learn the correct approach to piano playing from the beginning, so that many of the problems that may occur through learning incorrect positions and movements can be avoided. Unfortunately, this almost never happens. Instead, pianists who become interested in the Taubman Approach generally fall into one of four groups. First are pianists who have tried many different treatments for their severe symptoms that didn't work and ultimately discover the Taubman Approach as a potential solution to their problems. Second are those who begin to notice symptoms, see the handwriting on the wall, and start looking for help. The third group includes pianists who experience limitations and desire to go beyond their current level. They want to play pieces that previously felt unplayable, improve their ability to play rapidly and evenly with ease and security, and enhance their general expressivity. Finally, there are pianists who have heard about the Approach, are curious, and want a taste of the work. For all these individuals, I suggest an initial commitment of at least two lessons, closely spaced in time, since one lesson is usually not enough to experience noticeable change.

DIFFERENCES IN ABILITIES AND ATTITUDES

Some pianists can concentrate better and absorb information more rapidly than others. On a physical level, students vary in their sensitivity to the "feel" of their playing apparatus when experiencing these new positions and movements. Due to individual differences in their mental and physical capabilities, students vary in their ability to translate the words of the teacher into the desired physical actions. As a result, students advance at different rates. Ideally, the student needs to be open to learning, since it is necessary to put aside long-held beliefs in order to absorb new information. Also, curiosity leads to becoming involved and interested in the process instead of focusing only on the end result. This enables a student to progress more rapidly.

PRACTICE

When one is first learning basic principles of coordinate movement, five- or ten-minute sessions at the piano are sufficient. Learning a small amount of material at a time is more effective than trying to assimilate a lot of information all at once.

After the student has absorbed and incorporated the various elements of the technique and new pieces are added, the practice sessions increase in length. The transformed technique allows the student to learn pieces more rapidly, to retain what has been learned more fully, to use practice time to concentrate on the musical aspects of a piece, and to learn new pieces.

FREQUENCY OF LESSONS

Another important factor in the pace of learning and implementing new ideas and habits is the frequency of lessons. In the beginning, a great deal of information must be learned to establish a solid basis, so regular guidance is necessary. A few days of practice are normally sufficient for the student to absorb the material from the previous lesson. At that point the teacher can determine if it is time to add the next step, or if the student needs to stay with the material already presented. Short lessons twice a week are ideal at the beginning, and weekly lessons are the minimum necessary for good progress. When lessons are spaced out to every two to three weeks, progress is generally slower.

OBSTACLES TO ACQUIRING A NATURAL PIANO TECHNIQUE

Several obstacles can impede a natural piano technique, some through no fault of the pianist.

1. Most of the motions in a coordinate technique are invisible and may seem counterintuitive at first.

2. As the Taubman Approach has become more known, many unqualified Taubman teachers claim to be experts. However, teaching that results from insufficient training is generally ineffective, and can even lead

to more problems. Even worse, it compromises the credibility of the Approach and its transformative power.

3. Some people find it more difficult to change longstanding habits than others.

4. There are also many mistruths and clichés about the Taubman Approach.

IMPERCEPTIBLE DIFFERENCES

As I have noted throughout the book, the motions that govern correct piano technique are for the most part invisible. The Taubman Approach is based on the realization that the motions that make piano playing natural and effective are mostly hidden from the eye. Ralph Waldo Emerson described this phenomenon best when he said, "Nothing is rich but the inexhaustible wealth of nature. She shows us only surfaces, but she is a million fathoms deep" (1904). Since these motions are mostly imperceptible, they were extremely difficult to decipher. The genius of Dorothy Taubman was her realization that the visible movements of the fingers were only the tip of the iceberg, and the gift of the Taubman Approach is the discovery of these mostly invisible motions, their functions, and their importance.

As a result of traditional reliance on the visible aspects of piano playing, the norms in the field have included practicing with isolated fingers, stretching exercises, dropping the wrist, and practicing repetitively and endlessly. The proliferation of injuries in the field demonstrates the inefficacy and flaws of these norms.

COUNTERINTUITIVE MOVEMENTS

Correct piano technique is often counterintuitive. What is considered natural and intuitive may often be merely habit developed over years of practice.

According to scientist Carl Sagan, "Our intuition is by no means an infallible guide. Our perceptions may be distorted by training and prejudice or merely because of the limitations of our sense organs, which, of course, perceive but a small fraction of the world" (1979, 13). Only when the positions and motions of the playing apparatus are used correctly does piano playing become intuitive, easy, efficient, and symptom-free. In most cases, these positions and movements have to be taught. Once the pianist begins to experience improvement, what seemed counterintuitive starts to become natural.

QUALIFIED AND UNQUALIFIED TEACHERS

As mentioned previously, if the teacher who is teaching this approach is not properly trained or sufficiently experienced, results may be minimal or nonexistent, and preexisting problems may even worsen. The student who studies with an unqualified teacher may obtain some relief, yet continue to have problems and lose hope. In contrast, the effective Taubman teacher is well trained in all aspects of the Taubman Approach, with the ability to diagnose problems and offer solutions. Ultimately, the quality of the teacher is demonstrated through his or her results: effective Taubman teachers consistently transform their students' playing.

CHANGING HABITS

Human beings tend to resist change, even when the status quo causes suffering. Without change, suffering continues, regardless of whether it's from our personal relationships, foods that are bad for us, or drugs that poison our minds and bodies.

Pianists often experience fatigue, tension, and pain. In fact, sometimes the pain can be so severe that it results in the inability to play or perform, which in turn leads to loss of self-esteem, breakdowns, depression, and even suicide. These problems are not inevitable. They are simply caused by wrong habits at the piano, which can be changed at any age and level. The first step to making a change is to question and understand the root cause of the problem. The Taubman teacher provides the solution, but understanding, determination and patience on the part of the student are necessary for the new, correct habits to take root and feel natural.

CLICHÉS AND PREJUDICES

Clichés abound in the field of piano instruction, and incorrect clichés can easily derail learning. For example, one slogan we often hear is "practice makes perfect." Nevertheless, we spend hours and years at the piano, yet often with little progress to show for our efforts. Other clichés that can prevent progress and prolong suffering are:

1. "No pain, no gain."
2. "Discomfort and injuries are inevitable."
3. "There are as many techniques as pianists."
4. "Repetitive stress injuries result from overuse."
5. "These symptoms are all in your head."

In addition, prejudices about the Taubman Approach itself are:

1. "It takes forever to learn."
2. "It results in a poor sound."
3. "It leads to everyone sounding the same."
4. "Analyzing technique eliminates the magic of music."
5. "It's all about large rotation, and it's impossible to play fast that way."

Although these clichés abound, they can be easily dispelled by taking a series of lessons with a qualified Taubman teacher who has information tailored to addressing specific problems.

TAUBMAN APPROACH PEDAGOGICAL INSIGHTS

The Taubman Approach is primarily experiential. How the new movements feel to the student is a guide for both teacher and student. The teacher constantly asks, "How does it feel?" and the student's feedback helps the teacher know how to proceed. Traditionally, students are told that if they practice enough, they will achieve the desired results. However, in the Taubman Approach repetition is valuable only if the pianist is repeating the correct motions learned in the lesson.

When the student is playing well, isn't experiencing symptoms, and wants to understand a larger picture of the technique, that's the right time to explain the wider context. This allows the student to become more independent in analyzing and solving problems. Also, as these new movements become incorporated into the hands, the teacher's additional explanations can further improve playing by giving the student more control and more understanding of what is taking place.

For students to learn successfully, it helps to teach the material in small increments, since in most cases the brain can best absorb only a small amount of information at one time.

In the beginning, when students ask if exercises for developing muscles are still necessary, they are surprised to hear that no exercises are needed. This runs counter to their experience over many years. Instead, the Taubman Approach initially teaches a magnified and slower version of a technique comprised of different elements that result in speed. Once fully learned and integrated, these elements together become a natural and effective piano technique, with the speed and ease required to play pieces that were previously out of reach.

Finally, it is extremely important to teach students only what they need in order to solve their particular problems. An expert teacher knows what to bring to the student's consciousness and even more importantly, what not to say. It is not always necessary to teach every motion, since correct motions often produce other correct motions without the pianist even realizing it. When I first started studying with Dorothy Taubman, I didn't realize that I was learning only the specific information necessary to solve my own technical limitations. At the end of my first year with her, she invited me to a lecture in which she gave an overview of her approach. I was dumbfounded to find out that there was so much more to it than what I had been learning. Only later did I understand that the Approach has so many facets that initially students receive only what they need to resolve their own particular problems.

INITIAL CONTACT AND FIRST LESSON

Prior to their initial meeting with me, prospective students describe their studies, the technical issues they are confronting, and what they hope to achieve. They ask what to bring and how much to prepare for the first lesson. I tell them to bring a short example of something they consider easy to play and another example of something that gives them trouble. If they are in pain, I tell them not to practice until they see me. I encourage them to come with questions and to be prepared to discuss their symptoms.

It helps if students have some prior knowledge of the fundamental concepts of the Taubman Approach. Then I don't need to spend time introducing basic principles in the first lesson, but can immediately begin to show how to implement principles.

At the first lesson, I continue to investigate the student's condition and abilities. To address their problems, I ask when and where they felt a change for the worse. Was it in a particular piece of music? A particular passage?

A particular aspect of technique? Was it the left hand, the right hand, or both? I ask if there was a time when the playing felt good and natural, or whether they always felt tension and limitations. Common complaints are difficulties in playing rapid scale passages, arpeggios, trills, leaps, chords, octaves, and broken octaves, playing loudly and softly, and the inability to produce a singing tone.

I then ask the student to play a page or two, or a whole piece if they wish; this shows me the underlying reasons for the problems. Because some of the sources of problems may be invisible and can only be located and resolved through continued exploration, it is best to start with the most obvious and problematic issues. I ask the student about their symptoms and location, even though the physical location of the symptoms does not always indicate the root cause of the problem. I write down their technical history and other important facts about their training and refer to these notes as they progress, along with the steps that I take to correct the problems.

I also check the student's typing habits on the computer and smartphone, as well as their handwriting. Poor habits when using these devices (e.g., stretching, twisting, curling, and finger isolation) are major contributing factors to problems at the piano and must be corrected. Conversely, symptoms from incorrect piano playing often affect computer use and other activities of daily living that involve the hands. I check these activities as well, since incorrect usage in these areas will slow down resolution of problems at the piano.

Occasionally, pianists come to me with injuries so severe that their entire relationship to the instrument is damaged. One pianist came to me with his hands frozen in midair, so that he couldn't even get to the keyboard without experiencing symptoms. My first task was to reestablish his relationship with the instrument. I closed the keyboard lid, put a pencil on the music rack, and asked him to pick up a pencil, which he did easily. As long as he wasn't thinking about the keyboard, his hand behaved normally. I then opened the lid and told him to approach the keyboard just as if it were any other surface in daily life. This simple instruction was the gateway to normalizing his relationship to the piano. It helped to reestablish a relationship with the keyboard that was free of anxiety.

When normalcy is restored, I begin to work on the specific causes of an injury in order to resolve it. The teacher's expertise is an essential aspect of this process. A little Taubman knowledge is like knowing a few words in a foreign language: until you learn enough, it is difficult to communicate.

SUBSEQUENT LESSONS

Students often report that one forgotten instruction from the lesson made a big difference in their practicing that week. Since it is impossible to remember all the details given during the session, most people record their lessons. The recording is a helpful reference tool between lessons and helps the student to practice efficiently, since practicing in the Taubman Approach means practicing the information that was presented in the lesson. I encourage the student to write down solutions in the score such as fingering, shaping, in-and-out motions and more. I also ask people to write down their questions between lessons. These questions may relate to issues from the previous lesson or any other area. Aside from the Taubman Approach's treasure trove of information and the results achieved through putting that information into practice, the fact that questioning was encouraged drew me to it from the very beginning. If my practice during the week didn't resolve a problem completely, I would bring it back to the next lesson, repeat my question, and obtain more information until the problem was fully resolved and I could play the passage securely and automatically. In this way, I was able to learn faster without having to practice endlessly.

THE PROCESS OF BECOMING A TAUBMAN TEACHER

Over the years, as I continued to improve my skills to teach this work more and more effectively, I realized that to be a good Taubman teacher requires training, and I established the Professional Training Program at the Golandsky Institute for that purpose. In this concluding section I address the process required to become a certified Taubman teacher.*

To successfully learn how to teach correct piano technique, the pianist must first resolve their own pianistic problems and then become well trained in all the other aspects of the Taubman Approach as well. Private lessons with a knowledgeable Taubman teacher and exposure to written material, videos, and workshops on the Approach are essential. Then, while continuing their own pianistic development, the pianist learns through experience and observation how to diagnose problems and implement solutions for other pianists. To accomplish this, the student works with their own students under the mentoring of the master teacher over an extended period of time. To become certified as a Taubman teacher by the Golandsky Institute, the prospective teacher must be able to demonstrate theoretical knowledge of the Approach, to accurately diagnose all types of problems in students, and to implement and communicate solutions effectively to a wide variety of people with different abilities, backgrounds, and problems.

Additionally, the committed Taubman teacher must continue with both personal pianistic development and pedagogical development, especially considering the increasing frequency and severity of piano injuries today. Teachers with the Golandsky Institute can be certified at three levels of proficiency: instructor, associate, and master teacher.

All the obstacles to learning correct piano technique also apply to pianists

* For information on how to become a Golandsky Institute certified teacher, go to https://www.golandskyinstitute.org/professional-training-program/

who want to become teachers. However, the process delineated above demonstrates that learning to teach the Taubman Approach requires more skills, time, and commitment than simply studying for one's own benefit.

CONCLUSION

I wrote this book to ensure that the extensive body of knowledge that Dorothy Taubman discovered and developed would be properly documented. I also wanted to include some of my own insights, which have contributed to making the work even more effective and accessible. Pianists most often come to the Approach with problems that seem unsolvable. With lessons, they are not only able to resolve their problems, but acquire skills and efficiency they never imagined possible. The Taubman Approach has made unlimited growth and improvement realistic for pianists of all ages and abilities.

I am hugely gratified by the fact that there is a whole new generation of pianists who are inspired by their own improvement, and want to pass this knowledge on to others as well. It gives me hope that one day we will live in a pain-free world when it comes to playing the piano and its sister instruments.

In closing, I would like to share testimonials written by students whom I have taught. These testimonials speak to the transformative power of the Taubman Approach.

Lisa Yui

DMA, Manhattan School of Music. Concert pianist, lecturer, teacher, author, and faculty member of the Manhattan School of Music and the Juilliard School Extension Division.

Working with Edna Golandsky has been one of the most transformative events of my musical life. I was introduced to Edna following years of hand injuries that reached a point of canceling concerts. At our first lesson, she said two things that blew my mind: "You should be able to practice for as long as you like without pain" and "If you fail more than twice to play a passage the way you want, you're doing something wrong." These statements went against what I had been taught until then—that piano technique was related to strength and stamina, and that success could not be achieved without repetition and, at times, pain. I worked with Edna many times since that first meeting, often on passages where I couldn't achieve the desired effect, or simply seemed impossible to play.

It would be no exaggeration to say that she always, always, found a solution, at times so elegantly simple that I would wonder how the passage ever troubled me to begin with. What Edna taught me was that pain is never good, and that there is a solution to every technical challenge. This should give hope to every pianist.

Yegor Shevtsov

DMA, Manhattan School of Music. Pianist with the Arctic Philharmonic, Boda, Norway.

I am a working pianist, and I owe that honor in no small measure to Edna's precise, encouraging, and constructive teaching. Both she and her wonderful colleagues at the Institute are an incredible resource to pianists of all levels, from beginner students to those wishing to recover from injury to those who simply look to be better pianists, better musicians. I came to Edna to get help with very practical and concrete problems: I needed to perform some pieces that I could not play well. Over the years, I have brought to her Chopin and Scriabin etudes for gigs, Beethoven and Brahms sonatas for competitions, Strauss and Stravinsky orchestral excerpts for auditions.

From fingerings to articulation, from sound quality to rhythmic vitality—Edna leaves no stone unturned. What separates her from other teachers is of course the fact that she enables you to explore all those categories as rooted in the anatomical evidence of playing the instrument. Through studying with her, I have become not just a better performer, but a better musician and a better teacher myself. Edna is an embodiment of a Master Teacher. Thank you, Master.

Friar Sean Duggan

MFA, Carnegie Mellon. Pianist, competition winner, and professor at SUNY Fredonia, New York.

Edna Golandsky is the most wonderful piano teacher I have ever worked with. Her patience and persistence clearly communicate to the student through words and demonstrations of what the student most needs to hear and understand. Her amazing insight and her master classes go directly to the musical and, if necessary, technical issues at hand and enable the student to play a piece better than he/she ever thought possible. She is particularly brilliant at dealing with sound production, rhythm, and musical structure.

I continue to see Edna from time to time to realign and refine my technique. Thanks to her, I can now play repertoire I never thought I could approach. In addition, I can now play my own music with a sound that previously existed only in my imagination.

Thomas Bagwell

Faculty member, Mannes School of Music and formerly Yale University, Collaborative Pianist and Assistant Conductor, Metropolitan Opera, Washington Opera, and Santa Fe Opera, and currently at the Copenhagen Opera House.

Before I studied with Edna Golandsky, I had tremendous shoulder pain, and my sound was weak. I felt that my technique had gone as far as it could go and that there was no hope for improvement. As a result of working with Edna, my pain is gone. In addition, my tone, and my ability to express music are far better than I ever thought they could be. I was able to make these changes in spite of the fact that I had to continue playing all the while to earn a living.

Edna's brilliant teaching is so understandable that when you come in with a problem, you're always going to leave with a solution other than "just practice it more." She pushes you to go further with your talent and inspires you to be a complete musician. In short, Edna's teaching has opened more doors in my playing than I knew were there.

Ilya Itin

Professor of piano, faculty member, Musashino Academy, Tokyo. Concert pianist and Leeds Competition gold medalist.

Edna Golandsky is a consummate expert of piano technique and musical artistry. The depth of her analytical ability surpasses anything I have encountered. Her work frees performers, enabling them to realize their full potential.

Danilo Perez

Founder and artistic director of Berklee Global Jazz Institute, renowned jazz pianist, Grammy Award winner, composer, producer, and educator.

Before I met Edna I always had to warm up. Now I can sit at the piano and just go. I never get uncomfortable or tired. Even when I am away from the piano, when I come back, I can play right away. I understand how to get every color, be it singing, percussive, or anything in between.

This education should be taught worldwide. It should be a part of every educational system from early on so pianists can develop to their utmost potential. It makes playing the piano so easy. It has also made me a much better listener to the degree that I can help the tuner do a better job with the different pianos that I perform on. I am so aware now of the evenness of the keys and of the sound.

Edna Golandsky's work with the Taubman method allowed me to reflect and learn as a musician—she woke up my awareness of the subtleties and beauties of tone production.

Arthur Simoes

BA, MA, Haute Ecole de Musique, Geneva. Pianist.

I was born in Brazil and moved to Geneva, Switzerland, at age ten. I had an injury in both of my thumbs when I decided to attend the Golandsky Institute Summer Symposium at Princeton University for the first time in 2017. I had just graduated from the Haute Ecole de Musique in Geneva and my problems started while I was preparing for my Bachelor's recital. During the weeks preceding the symposium I had watched the ten DVDs and some videos from the Golandsky Streaming and I was absolutely fascinated with what I was learning. The private instruction that I had in Princeton further expanded my interest and my curiosity for the Taubman Approach.

At that time, despite my injury, I was preparing for the European Music Competition "Città di Moncalieri" in Italy. I decided to travel to New York for a week in October, one month before the competition, to have lessons with Edna Golandsky. I was amazed by the way she made passage after passage feel easy and secure in my hands. Fast forward one month, I was very happy to win the first prize at the competition, but I was still injured despite having gone through doctors and physical therapy. At that point I knew that I wanted to retrain my technique.

I was finally able to move to New York in October 2018 to study with Edna and that has probably been the best decision I've made in my life. I stayed until June 2019. The pain started disappearing after about three months, but that was only the beginning. I slowly started learning more advanced repertoire again and I could play with a sense of ease, security, and control that was completely new to me.

I continue my lessons to the present day. I rarely have to think about the technique; and whenever I am faced with a challenging passage, I feel empowered with the tools that I now have. Before, when I tried to play expressively, it was a struggle and I felt I was pushing. Now I feel that I have a choice in how to express the music, without just hoping that things will come out well.

I am eternally grateful to Edna for showing me the path to a healthier way of playing the piano, and therefore a happier and more fulfilled musical career.

Juan Lazaro

BM, The Juilliard School, MM, Manhattan School of Music, Lindemann Young Artist Program.

I have been studying with Edna privately for six years now and can say that I have achieved a level of ease, musicality, and understanding that I would have never arrived at without her. That knowledge was tested to very extreme limits when, in March, I had to perform a rigorous audition to enter the Metropolitan Opera's Lindemann program a week before an extremely risky surgery to fix a poorly executed upper arm fracture surgery from a year before. The moment the doctor cleared me for movement, I began to play like before, without any fear or limitation. Technique and understanding alone allowed me to bypass the crippling condition of my left arm and give a musical and sophisticated display of my abilities in a forty-minute audition. I was the only one accepted for the season and I owe it to the technical and musical knowledge passed on to me by Edna Golandsky.

Yaniv Dinur

PhD, conducting, University of Michigan. Concert pianist and conductor, Milwaukee and New Bedford Symphony Orchestras.

Prior to my lessons with Edna, playing the piano felt like combat. When I first came to her, I pointed to a passage that I'd been struggling with for years. Edna showed me a few things and I tried the passage again. She then asked her famous question, "How's that?"

I paused for a second and said: "So easy!" She said: "Imagine, with this technique, anything can feel like that."

Since then, every lesson with Edna has been a revelation. She shares her broad knowledge with love and generosity, combined with a laid-back approach and a sense of humor. Thanks to her, I have managed to play pieces that I never dreamed I would be able to. She changed my life.

Josu De Solaun

DMA, Manhattan School of Music, Enescu Competition gold medalist, concert pianist, and recording artist.

I studied the Taubman Approach intensively with Edna Golandsky for three years, from 2009 to 2012, almost every week. The knowledge I gained, not only about what I was doing right at the piano, but about the many areas of improvement in my craft at the instrument, will serve me for the rest of my life. She opened up large vistas and horizons as to the possibilities of both the piano and of my own abilities using it to make music.

Edna is a vast repository of the most sophisticated biomechanical knowledge about how to play the instrument beautifully. Nothing I could say could do justice to the scope and subtlety of her deep understanding of this our beloved instrument, of our bodies, and of the intricate relationships between them.

Sylvie Courvoisier

Jazz pianist, composer, improviser. Faculty member, New School. Winner, German Jazz Prize Keyboards International, 2022.

I first met Edna Golandsky in 2003 at the Taubman Symposium in Amherst, Massachusetts. I was looking for solutions to technical problems I had at the time, so that I could translate my musical ideas to the instrument without barriers. I was really impressed by the master classes that Edna gave, the clarity of her approach to solving problems on the piano, her musical concepts, her tone, and how she explained the value of natural alignment in the body to achieve a full sound without having to strain in ways that would develop body pain and/or fatigue.

When I returned from the symposium, I decided to take private lessons with Edna, and over time worked on the entire Taubman technique with her. Edna is fantastic; in addition to resolving the problems I had at that time, she also gave me the tools to solve any pianistic issues I might encounter. I have enthusiastically recommended Edna to many colleagues. She is the best teacher I have ever had.

Kat Sherrell

Multidisciplinary musician, composer, musical director, and author.

I started studying with a student of Edna's and then Edna soon after I first started playing rehearsals for a Broadway show, my first true professional-level gig. The score was notoriously challenging, and I was having trouble learning the music fast enough and playing consistently (sometimes I played brilliantly, sometimes not, and I never felt like I could predict or control what was going to come out under pressure). Also, I was suffering from nerves, and felt the kind of fatigue I was afraid would lead to injury, as well as some pain in my thumbs and fifth fingers.

Edna got down to the fundamental problems in my technique, problems other teachers had brushed off or been unable to explain when I asked questions. I very quickly noticed significant improvements in my playing, my ability to sight-read and learn music quickly, and the way my hands felt.

While Edna's background is classical, her deep understanding of music has helped me in my playing of pop and Broadway repertoire as well as my ability to handle technically demanding scores.

I would probably not be playing today without the Taubman Approach and the work Edna has done to build on it. But with their help, over the past few years I've been able to build my reputation as a pianist/keyboardist in the Broadway community, and I'm able to handle the workload and the pressure that comes along with great opportunities, because my skills are so much more solid.

Therese Milanovic

PhD, Queensland Conservatorium, Griffith University. Master teacher, Golandsky Institute.

My first introduction to the Taubman Approach was in 2003, followed by a four-year gap before I was able to afford to return to the USA from my hometown of Brisbane, Australia. Those first lessons with Edna Golandsky in 2007 were nothing short of revelatory. With her help, I overcame my nearly decade-long injury, and was so thrilled to be playing at all that I had reconciled the many technical limitations in my playing as inevitable. Through those initial exhilarating lessons with Edna at the Golandsky Institute Summer Symposium, I quickly began to understand that there was a concrete, logical answer to every one of my unending list of questions.

After my experience of nearly a decade-long injury with seemingly little help available, it was also clear (and shocking to me) that overcoming injury was merely the first stage in the deep learning possible through the Taubman Approach. A seed of hope grew that through studying this knowledge, I might one day be able to reach a higher level of facility and artistry. Little did I know how much my playing and life path would be enriched by the learning ahead.

Since then, I have had the great fortune of several intensive study periods in New York City with Edna, traveled to NYC a dozen times, and bridged the thousands of miles between us with many wonderful online lessons since 2009, for which I am ever grateful. Through Edna's masterful skills, I have been able to pursue the possibility of pursuing a pathway in music to the fullest, and now lead a rich and full life of teaching and disseminating the Taubman Approach and performing at a high level with wonderful musicians that I adore.

As my playing has developed over the course of our careful, detailed work together, I have not only been able to perform increasingly difficult repertoire, but to be completely present to the music when performing. The performance anxiety that I previously struggled with has long since dissolved.

It is an incredible feeling to walk onto the stage, feeling secure that every obstacle has been thoroughly worked through, and that the performance can be just as secure as in the practice room, allowing my attention to be solely focused on responding to and shaping the music. As our work together has deepened, it has been a great joy to experience and understand the indivisible nature of technique and artistry, and that these elements that were previously somewhat mystical or unreliable for me are in fact learnable and teachable.

I have also been extremely fortunate to observe many hours of Edna's life-changing teaching, from putting severely injured students back together step-by-step with kindness and deep patience, to working with incredible artists at the highest level seeking to develop their capacity still further. I will also never forget the lessons I observed with Edna and Sophie Till, witnessing Edna's brilliant, agile, and flexible thinking in developing an equally profound and far-reaching pedagogical system of understanding for stringed instruments. Over the years, I have received invaluable feedback in presenting my own students, with many memorable moments of Edna skillfully navigating them through gnarly, complex situations through to transformational breakthroughs. I deeply value her ongoing mentoring, guidance, and friendship.

The most profound learning for me through my studies with Edna is that there is always hope, even when hope is lost, and there is always an answer, albeit some more layered than others. Her skill, intuition, and insight based on experience combined with formidable musicianship has been an ongoing model to aspire to, and certainly the inspiration for me to work so hard to attain certification with the Golandsky Institute and bring this vital body of knowledge to my country. I look forward to many more years of our work together, and as always, am excited and curious as to what the next lesson might reveal. Even after all these years, the solutions can still be surprising, and I am thrilled to discover new learnings in each lesson.

Yuri Aoki

Graduate, Lindemann Young Artist Development Program. Collaborative pianist and vocal coach.

My experience with Ms. Golandsky took place when I was a member of the Lindemann Young Artist Development Program at the Metropolitan Opera, as a pianist in training who specializes mainly in opera and other vocal repertoire.

I had been trained from an early age in Japan with a technique focused on finger isolation, and as I was deepening my studies for the opera repertoire, I had experienced several episodes of tendonitis, and had believed that my body was simply not cut out to play this music with ease, due to my petite build and the lack of "power." I had been treated to several steroid injections in my wrist, only to be disappointed by the pain that would attack me again several years later. I had always lived with the fear of having to stop doing the work that I love with all my heart due to the imminent chronic injury.

Working with Ms. Golandsky was for me a transformative experience, both physically and mentally. Through her work and philosophy, not only my technique but also my mindset had been completely transformed. Aside from the obvious physical aspects, one of the greatest gifts from her was the experience of learning how to be non-judgmental—as she said to me in my first lesson, "nothing is wrong with you"—and that when encountering a problem, one should observe it with specificity and generosity, and proceed while accepting the state of the mind, the brain, and the body, and guiding them gently to do their work in the most natural, efficient way. Before I worked with Ms. Golandsky, I had believed that learning and improving my performance should be a painful process—always a war with my misperceived physical incapability, and also lack of confidence. I would often discover that a "bad habit" was a result of physical and/or mental trauma that I had imposed on myself in the history of my playing, and uncovering and learning from my own background through Ms. Golandsky's guidance was a fascinating experience.

I had countless eye-opening moments in my work with her—but I will never forget that moment when I played an octave chord with both hands for the first time under her guidance. I felt like I had made absolutely no physical effort, the sound itself was so deep, beautiful, and released, and I felt like I was being gently embraced by the piano and the beauty of its natural sonority. It was a sensation I had never experienced in all my twenty-five years of piano playing.

Without Ms. Golandsky's work and dedication, I would not be where I am today—fearless, because I now know that there is always a way. Words fail to express my gratitude for her, and I sincerely encourage anyone to approach her technique who believes that they deserve pain in order to do what they love.

Jin Jeon

BM, MM, piano performance. Faculty member, Berlin Hanns Eisler School of Music.

I've always been eager to know more about playing the piano and classical music. When I was seventeen, I decided to move to the birthplace of classical music: Europe. Fortunately, I was accepted as the youngest applicant to the Hanns Eisler School of Music in Berlin. However, in the very last semester of my bachelor's program, my hands got seriously injured. At that time, I thought it was normal since I practiced almost nine hours a day in order to prepare for my bachelor concert. My teacher even suggested a break for a couple of weeks, but the pain was persistently there. Consequently, I had to take a semester off, went back to Korea, and took all kinds of medical treatments such as acupuncture, physiotherapy, and other conventional therapies. The break led to improvements and relief, but as soon as I started with intensive practice, the pain came unfortunately again, and the condition of my hand got even worse.

In retrospect, this has been the toughest time of my life. I was afraid that was the end of my future as a musician. On top of that, I even considered changing my profession.

However, every cloud has a silver lining, and as most turning points in life come out of the blue, I came across Taubman's approach on the internet. Coincidentally, I was told that Ms. Golandsky was coming to Turkey for a workshop in the next few months. I was desperate for a solution and flew to Istanbul without any further consideration. Just after the first lesson with Ms. Golandsky, I was very sure that I found the solution for my pain and desperation. After my graduation in Berlin, I moved to NYC to study with her and my pain surprisingly disappeared within a few months and never came back again.

Ms. Golandsky is a world-renowned expert on the Taubman Approach. Her experience, insights, and professional guidance helped me to understand how to play without pain and how to prevent it from recurring. Moreover, through intensive lessons with her, I could not only cure my hands but also open the door for endless possibilities of growth in my technique. That growth includes the ability to produce any sound I want, to shape phrases, to express rhythmic pulsation, and more. In other words, I'm learning how to use the technique to express music in a way that I've never been able to do before and I enjoy practicing and playing the piano with great ease and security.

Ms. Golandsky has substantially changed my life as a musician and my relationship with the piano. Furthermore, as I continue my work with her, I have been certified by the Golandsky Institute and find myself helping many students and pianists who are experiencing serious limitations as well as fatigue, tension, and pain. This makes me feel immensely grateful! I'm sincerely thankful for Ms. Golandsky's endless support and teaching and hope that this incredible work can flourish even more in the future so that fewer people suffer while playing the piano.

Deren Eryilmaz

Pianist and Taubman teacher.

The people we meet in life always affect us in one way or another. We would like to meet only the good ones and escape the rest. If we are lucky enough, we might meet someone who changes our lives forever. For me, that person is Edna Golandsky.

I met Edna when I was a teacher at one of the best conservatories of my country, training very talented pupils to become professional pianists. I was also Erasmus Program and Performance Organization coordinator of the faculty. Thirty years old, I was feeling at the peak of my career, that I reached my limit as a pianist, playing as a soloist with the orchestras and doing chamber music as much as my busy academic schedule permitted me. I was never injured but felt limited. Lost the ease I had when I was a young prodigy, but I was hoping to grow wiser as a teacher with the experience. I thought that was something that would happen in time. I didn't know I could have ten equally strong and able fingers, and I never guessed that all my questions had straightforward answers. I couldn't imagine that with the right teacher I could become one of the few teachers who could cure and help her students to overcome their limitations. The journey continues and every lesson is another step to get closer to pure joy and ease.

Thanks to Edna, the worst time of my life became the best and I was born again from my ashes. Now I can fly as high as I wish, while helping others to fulfill their dreams as well. As many of us who have had the pleasure to work with her feel, my only regret is not to have met her earlier. I will be forever grateful.

Leo Gorelkin

MD.

My wife, Paula, a classically trained pianist, playing the piano for fifty-three years, had received cortisone shots about three years ago and eventually surgery on both hands for three fingers from very painful and incapacitating injuries (trigger fingers) which apparently resulted from her playing. After the surgery, yet another finger was threatening. At that time, she met a teacher at the Golandsky Institute who suggested she be evaluated by Edna Golandsky, a major proponent and master teacher of the Taubman Approach. She professed that Edna might be helpful with her problem. What to do? Stop playing the piano, expect more surgery, or see Edna?

Luckily, Paula chose to give the Taubman technique and Edna Golandsky a try. A momentous choice indeed, as she, Paula, is now playing some of the more demanding and technically difficult pieces of the solo piano repertoire. During this time, that finger that had been threatening has long since been silent and she even tells me excitedly that she can master, even more quickly, very difficult piano passages. There is no longer any discomfort in either hand or fingers.

Now, I'm not a motion specialist, hand specialist, or pianist, but I am a physician with a strong scientific background in research and it makes perfect sense to me that any repetitive and demanding motions which can be effected with putting the least if any stress into those motions and still get the job done with even greater efficiency is something of great value and importance. This appears to exactly be the case using the Taubman Approach to piano playing with a properly certified teacher at the helm.

Impressive results with the Taubman approach in relieving and preventing injuries and also facilitating greater accomplishment at the piano appears to me to be a gross understatement.

Video Examples Directory

To view in-depth video examples for all the chapters in this book visit:

www.ednagolandsky.com/book

Or you can just hold most mobile device cameras over the QR code below and they will instantly pull up the webpage for you:

BIBLIOGRAPHY

Bertensson, Sergei, Jay Lead, and Sophia Satina. *Sergei Rachmaninoff: A Lifetime in Music.* New York: New York University Press, 1956.

Degler, Terry. *Fiery Muse: Inspiration and the Spiritual Quest.* Toronto: Random House of Canada, 1976.

Ellington, Duke and Irving Mills. "It Don't Mean a Thing If It Ain't Got That Swing." Detroit: Brunswick Records, 1932 (record).

Emerson, Ralph Waldo. *The Complete Works of Ralph Waldo Emerson.* Boston: Houghton Mifflin, 1904.

Fink, Seymour. *Mastering Piano Technique.* Portland: Amadeus Press, 1992.

Franco, Giuliano. "Bernardino Ramazzini: The Father of Occupational Medicine." *American Journal of Public Health* 91, no. 9 (September 2001): 1382.

Gieseking, Walter and Karl Leimer. *Piano Technique.* New York: Dover Publications, 1972.

Golandsky, Edna. "The Art of Rhythmic Expression." Filmed 2014. Golandsky Institute, 1:41. https://www.golandskyinstitute.org/product/the-art-of-rhythmic-expression/

—. "The Forgotten Lines." Filmed 2006. Golandsky Institute. New York, New York: 2006.

Hasty, Christopher F. "Just in Time for More Dichotomies—A Hasty Response." *Music Theory Spectrum* 21, Issue 2 (Fall 1999): 275–93. https://doi.org/10.2307/745865

Holcman, Jan. *The Legacy of Chopin.* New York: Philosophical Library, 1954.

Jaques-Dalcroze, Emile. *Le Rythme, La Musique et l'éducation.* Zurich, Suisse: Edition Foetisch, 1965.

Klass, Perry, M.D. "Texting, Surfing, Studying?" *New York Times*. October 12, 2009.

Little, Meredith and Natalie Jenne. *Dance and the Music of J. S. Bach,* expanded, ed. Bloomington, IN: Indiana University Press, 2001.

Marsalis, Wynton. 2001. *Jazz: A Film by Ken Burns*. Episode 6.

Miller, G. A. "The Magical Number Seven, Plus or Minus Two: Some Limits on Our Capacity for Processing Information." *Psychological Review* 101, no. 2 (April 1994): 343–52. http://doi.org/10.1037/0033-295X.101.2.343.

Montparker, Carol. "Rediscovering Rachmaninoff: A Visit with Ruth Laredo." *Clavier* (September 1986): 13.

Ortmann, Otto. *Physiological Mechanics of Piano Technique: An Experimental Study of the Nature of Muscular Action as Used in Piano Playing and of the Effects Thereof upon the Piano Key and the Piano Tone.* New York: Dutton, 1929.

Ostwald, Peter. *Glenn Gould: The Ecstasy and Tragedy of Genius.* New York: W. W. Norton, 1998: 298.

Paderewski, Ignace Jan, and Mary Lawton. *The Paderewski Memoirs.* New York: Charles Scribner's Sons, 1938.

Phillip, Lillie. *Piano Technique.* New York: Dover Publications, 1982.

Randel, Don Michael, ed. *The Harvard Concise Dictionary of Music.* Cambridge, Mass: Belknap Press of Harvard University Press, 1978.

Schumann, Clara. *The Marriage Diary of Robert and Clara Schumann.* Translated by Peter Ostwald. Boston: Northeastern University Press, 1993.

Sagan, Carl. *Broca's Brain.* New York: Random House, 1979.

Sandor, Gyorgy. *On Piano Playing.* New York: Schirmer Books, 1981.

Taubman, Dorothy. "Taubman Motion Studies." Unpublished notes, in the possession of the author, 1965–1990.

Varro, Margit. *Dynamic Piano Teaching.* Hamburg: Simrock N. London, 1966.

GLOSSARY

abductors: muscles that spread the fingers apart

adductors: muscles that bring the fingers together

arching (of the thumb): curving the thumb outward from the top knuckle, in the opposite direction of curling

broken nail joint: collapse of the first nail joint

collapse: the caving in of a joint, which breaks the natural alignment necessary for coordinate motion

coordinate motion: movement that uses the parts of the body involved in a coordinated way to achieve their maximum mechanical advantage, with minimum effort for maximum results

curling: pulling in the fingers at the nail joints, which activates the long flexors. The flexor digitorum profundus is one of the long flexor muscles that cross from the forearm into the hand. It is activated when the fingertips are curling and its contraction can contribute to tightening in the fingers and forearm

double rotation: two motions, (1) the preparatory motion, which is a motion opposite to the direction that the previous finger played, and (2) the playing stroke, which is a swing back in the same direction that the previous note played

dual muscular pull: when the muscles move in opposite directions at the same time (e.g., flexing and extending simultaneously)

enslavement to notation: in legato playing, the attempt to physically connect notes that are uncomfortable or impossible to physically connect

extensors: muscles that lift the fingers, hand, and forearm

fingertip pluck: in staccato playing, a small action of the fingertip at the bottom of the key that sends the playing apparatus to the next key without tension

flexors: muscles that move the fingers, hand, and forearm downward

forearm: the part of the arm that extends from the wrist to the elbow

forearm rotation: a turning of the forearm along with the hand and fingers, which (together with the walking hand and arm) allows the fingers to move across to the next key without isolating and stretching

fulcrum: a fixed point (e.g., a joint) from which movement occurs

grouping: organizing long and complex passages into smaller chunks of notes in order to simplify playing for greater fluency and security in speed, either through mental organization or physical breaks, in order to organize and simplify playing for greater fluency and security in speed

high bridge: when the top finger knuckles are too high, limiting the ability of the fingers to flex and abduct

in- and out-arrows: markings that indicate movement in toward the fallboard and out toward the body

interdependence: the interconnection of the two hands as they play together so that they become one kinetic experience

keybedding: excessive pressure applied at the bottom of the key

long flexors: muscles extending from the fingertip to the elbow that tighten the fingers, hand, wrist, and forearm when activated by curling

main finger knuckles: the top knuckles from which the fingers move

minimizing rotation: gradually decreasing the size of rotation until it is hardly felt or seen

overshaping: a forearm movement that creates an elliptical wave that gets initially higher and then lower over a group of notes

pianist: anyone, of any age or level, who plays the piano

playing apparatus: the fingers, hand, and forearm

point of sound: the point in the piano key, about three-eighths of an inch below the surface, where the hammer strikes the string

preparatory motion: the turning of the playing apparatus opposite to the direction that the next finger plays

rotation (see *forearm rotation*)

shaping: the adjustment of the forearm over long and short fingers that creates curvilinear lines

single rotation: when the fingers rotate in opposite directions and the preparatory motion is in the same direction as the last finger played

tone: the different qualities of sound that the piano can produce based on the pianist's use of weight and speed in striking the key

twisting: sideways movement of the hand at the wrist joint, either to the right or the left

undershaping: a forearm movement that creates an elliptical wave that gets initially lower and then higher over a group of notes

upper arm: the part of the arm that extends from the elbow to the shoulder

walking hand and arm: a sideways and up-and-down motion of the hand and forearm that together with rotation allows the fingers to move horizontally without stretching and provides the weight necessary to play each key

ACKNOWLEDGMENTS

My deepest gratitude goes to the many people whose help and support have made this book possible.

Ken Gorfkle worked with me on the book from the beginning to the end. As my "editor-in-chief," he not only helped me with editing and proofreading, but also made helpful suggestions throughout the entire writing process. His commitment to the value of this work and to the importance of making this information available to the general public has been unwavering and his support has been invaluable.

Therese Milanovic made many excellent and insightful suggestions and additions that helped to clarify many of the complex topics in the book and improved its readability.

My student Jin Jeon led the team of my students that organized the examples. He was selfless in his devotion, worked with great attention to all the aspects of this project, and was always available when I needed his help. Hugo Bermúdez was extremely helpful in this area as well, along with Ricky Moreira, Matthew Camastro, Dimitris Kostopoulos, Arthur Simoes, and Victor Montiel.

John Bloomfield, Robert Durso, and Mary Moran, co-founders of the Golandsky Institute, proofread my draft and offered useful suggestions.

Ira Rosenblum edited the Preface when I was first imagining the book.

Joseph Patrych videotaped and Asaf Blasberg edited the examples.

Alex Yagupsky engraved the musical scores into the examples.

My publicist, Sarah Parsons, helped in innumerable ways to bring the book to publication.

My beloved family, my children Amit and Galit, my daughter-in-law Tania, and my grand-daughters Miri, Naomi, Rachel, and Devorah, all gave me their love and support during the writing of the book.

Finally, I want to express my deepest appreciation and gratitude to my students and all the followers of the Taubman Approach, whose enthusiasm for the work motivated me to write this book and make this body of knowledge available to all.

ABOUT THE AUTHOR

Edna Golandsky is the leading exponent of the Taubman Approach. She has earned wide acclaim throughout the United States and abroad for her extraordinary ability to solve technical problems and for her penetrating musical insight. She received both her bachelor of music and master of music degrees from the Juilliard School, following which she continued her studies with Dorothy Taubman for over three decades.

Performers and students from around the world come to study, coach, and consult with Ms. Golandsky. A pedagogue of international renown, she has a long-established reputation for the expert diagnosis and treatment of problems such as fatigue, pain, and serious injuries, including carpal tunnel syndrome, tendonitis, focal dystonia, thoracic outlet syndrome, tennis and golfer's elbow, and ganglia. She has been a featured speaker at many music medicine conferences. She is an adjunct professor of piano at the City University of New York (CUNY). She is also currently serving on the faculty of the Lindemann Program of the New York Metropolitan Opera.

Ms. Golandsky has lectured and conducted master classes at some of the most prestigious music institutions in the United States, including the Eastman School of Music, Yale University, the Curtis Institute of Music, and Oberlin Conservatory. Internationally, she has given seminars in Canada,

Holland, Israel, Korea, Panama, and Turkey. In 2001, she was a guest lecturer at the European Piano Teachers' Association in Oxford, England, and in July 2003 she conducted a symposium in Lecce, Italy. In August 2010, she gave a master class and judged in a piano competition at the Chatauqua Festival. She was a guest presenter at the World Piano Pedagogy Conference in 2003 and 2009 and was engaged to return in October 2010. In 2011, she was a guest presenter at the Music Teachers National Association in Milwaukee, Wisconsin; the Piano Teachers Congress of New York; and the Music Teachers Association of California. She gave week-long workshops at the Panama Jazz Festival at 2009, 2010, 2012, and 2014. In 2012, she presented as a part of the New York University Steinhardt Master Class series and at the Music Teachers Association of California annual convention in San Diego.

For several years, Edna Golandsky worked with violinist, Sophie Till, who came seeking relief from long-standing problems. This has led to the development of a comprehensive application of the Taubman work to string instruments.

In the last few years, Edna Golandsky's activities have included workshops at the Forum Musikae festival in Spain, as well as in London, California, North Carolina, and multiple cities in China. She has given webinars with the Music Teachers National Association, the Music Teachers Association of California and Washington, a course to Master's degree students at the Musikeon in Madrid, a series of lectures on the leading classical music platform ToneBase, and virtual presentations to pianists and teachers around the world on a regular basis. She has been featured in publications such as the *New York Times*, the *Strad, Piano Magazine, Classical Music, Jazz Times*, and the *Clavier Companion*, among others.

Edna Golandsky is the person with whom Dorothy Taubman worked most closely. In 1976, Ms. Golandsky conceived the idea of establishing an Institute where people could come together during the summer and pursue an intensive investigation of the Taubman Approach. She encouraged Mrs.

Taubman to establish the Taubman Institute, which they ran together as co-founders. As the face of the Taubman Approach, Ms. Golandsky discusses each of its elements in a ten-volume video series. Mrs. Taubman has written, "I consider [Edna Golandsky] the leading authority on the Taubman Approach to instrumental playing."

In 2003, along with co-founders John Bloomfield, Robert Durso, and Mary Moran, Edna Golandsky founded The Golandsky Institute in order to expand the reach of the Taubman Approach through organizing year-round workshops and seminars for pianists and teachers. With her co-founders, she developed a Taubman Teacher Certification Program to standardize the expertise of Taubman teachers at the highest level possible. She and her co-founders also developed a highly successful streaming program to impart information on the Taubman Approach online to Taubman enthusiasts.

As Edna's knowledge deepened over the years, she continued to develop new instructional material. In conjunction with the Golandsky Institute, she has further developed the Taubman Approach in the three-DVD set, *The Art of Rhythmic Expression*, which has been praised worldwide; and the two-DVD set, *The Forgotten Lines: Lines that Support, Surround, and Intensify the Melody*. This material, along with the material that Edna has posted on her own website and on YouTube over the years, has been viewed by over a million pianists.